MADE FOR TRAVEL

MARY MULARI

Published by

Krause Publications

700 E. State St.
Iola, WI 54990-0001
Telephone 715-445-2214
www.krause.com

Please call or write for our free catalog of publications. Our toll-free number to place an order or obtain a free catalog is 800-258-0929 or please use our regular business telephone, 715-445-2214.

Photography by Don Hoffman, Rex McDonald Studio, Wadena, Minnesota
Illustrations by Mary Mulari

Library of Congress Catalog Number: 2001096288

ISBN: 0-87341-577-9

Printed in the United States of America

The following registered or trademarked company or product names appear in this book:
Iron Quick, Lycra, Polarfleece™, Sensuede™, Teflon, Ultrasuede®, Velcro®.

On the cover:

Bag Handle Wrap, page 78

Cosmetic Bag, page 33

Drawstring Jewelry Bag, page 31

Luggage Tag, page 76

Rug-ged Tote, page 53

Ice Cream Bucket Tote, page 72

Dedication

With great appreciation for their love and support, I dedicate this book to my new friends at the Thursday night meetings.

Acknowledgments

Every book I've written needed help from other people, and this book is no exception. It is a pleasure to recognize the individuals and companies that have come to my assistance.

The sewing machine companies and their representatives have always been ready to answer questions and provide help: BabyLock, Bernina, Brother, Elna, Janome, Pfaff, Singer, and Viking.

New products, fabrics, and notions have been provided by A & E, Amazing Designs, Dan River Inc., Fiskars, JHB International, Kunin Felt, Malden Mills, Marcus Brothers Textiles Inc., Oilcloth International, Prym Dritz, The RainShed Inc., Wrights, and YLI Corporation.

Nancy Zieman and the staff at Nancy's Notions continue to support and encourage my work and ideas. I have enjoyed the opportunities to present the information from my books as a frequent guest on *Sewing with Nancy* on PBS television and during numerous seminar appearances at Nancy's Notions Sewing Weekend Expo™.

Family and friends who cheer me on with their unending support and love have made a great difference in my life and in the process of writing this book during the summer of 2001.

Thanks to Don Hoffman for another great photography session. The inventive pictures in this book are a direct result of Don's creative ideas and talent with his cameras.

The staff and hospitality management group of The Lodge at Giants Ridge provided a wonderful place for the photography sessions. I'm proud to say that this fine resort hotel is located just minutes away from my home in Aurora, Minnesota. Special thanks to Holly Waisanen and Barb Starken.

Thanks to Susan Keller and to Barbara Case for their guidance and editorial assistance with this book.

All of you who have read my books, sewed the projects, and responded with enthusiasm and encouraging words have contributed to my success and my own level of enthusiasm for sewing and inventing new ideas for all of us to enjoy.

Safe and interesting journeys to all of you, along with my appreciation and sincere thanks.

Contents

Simple Stuff Sacks

Smart Storage Bags

Terrific Totes

Take-Along Accessories

Safe and Secure Bags

Accessories for the Beach and Beyond

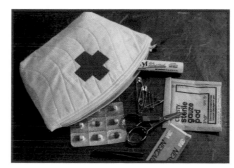

Traveling Kits

Introduction

Everyone travels. Daily, we leave our homes and need to carry things with us. Sometimes we leave on an extended trip to a faraway place and then we need secure bags to hold and hide a passport and credit cards. Students travel to college and need a laundry bag. Families head for the beach or pool with towels, bathing suits, and swim goggles stuffed in a mesh bag. Most people don't leave the house without some type of tote bag. In this book, you'll find projects for all of these journeys and more.

Welcome to a new collection of travel accessories! My longtime readers may remember *Travel Gear and Gifts to Make*, a book I self-published in 1993. With that book I discovered that my readers enjoy making travel gear as much as I do. We like to sew projects that are useful, quick to complete, and easy to personalize. We can find fabulous fabrics for travel accessories in our own personal fabric collections and create gifts for everyone we know. We're always looking for new ideas, so this book presents more accessories to sew.

If you are a beginner in sewing or returning to sewing after many years away, this book is for you too. It begins with basic information about supplies and techniques that are used for many of the projects. Since many projects need zippers, I've developed a super-easy way to sew them so you don't have to feel intimidated. You'll also notice that many projects are labeled "Sew Easy." In the introduction to each project, I've suggested types of fabrics to use, but don't let my suggestions limit your choices. Have fun experimenting and incorporating your own ideas into the bags, kits, and accessories. I know you'll hear many compli-

ments when you offer your creations as gifts.

When we sew, we can add details and features and decorations to make our projects more practical and personal. If you're a machine embroidery fan, add your designs to the totes and bags in this book. Don't miss the "Options" given for each project. The ideas and innovations there might inspire you to create new variations. Be sure to let me know what you've created from my ideas; it's exciting for me to find out what you've made. Write to me at Box 87, Aurora, MN 55705 or send email to mary@marymulari.com.

Sprinkled throughout the book are hints from people who travel. We can learn from each other and make all our trips more comfortable, safe, and enjoyable. If you have hints to share, please send them to me for possible use on my website www.marymulari.com. Here's hoping you'll enjoy making the projects in this book.

Valuable Tools and Timely Techniques

◆ VALUABLE TOOLS

You'll see the following supplies listed for many projects in this book. It's a great idea to have them on hand and to know how to use them. I have found that clear thread (also called invisible nylon thread), pinking shears, a bodkin, Velcro, a Teflon presser foot, a variety of sewing machine needle sizes, Ultrasuede scraps and strips, chalk markers, wash-away markers, and soap slivers are all necessary items in my sewing room, especially for the projects in this book.

Clear thread is available in two "colors" – clear (which looks white on the spool) and smoke (which looks gray). Clear works best on light and medium colored fabrics, while smoke blends best with dark colors. I use this thread as both top and bobbin thread and find that I save sewing time because I don't have to change thread colors for every different fabric color. Unlike the earlier versions that resembled stiff fishing line, this thread is easy to handle and use. Be sure to add this thread to your spool collection.

Pinking shears save time with trimming and clipping seam allowances. They're also

Valuable Tools for the projects in Made for Travel: *bodkin, tape measure, clear thread, Teflon presser foot, rotary cutter and mat, soap for marking, Ultrasuede strips, pins, and pinking shears.*

useful for finishing fabric edges. Look at the edges of the Postcard Portfolio on page 40. Rotary cutters with wavy or pinked edges can also be used for trimming fabric edges. The Blanket in a Pillow project on page 68 is an example of using a decorative edge rotary cutter.

Use a **bodkin** to thread cord or ribbon through a casing. (Fig. 1) This simple little

bodkin

tool grips the end of the cord, then slides easily through a casing. A safety pin can also be used for threading cord but once you try a bodkin, you'll appreciate how quickly and easily a drawstring can be led through a casing.

Where would we be without **Velcro**? We can thank the space industry for the development of this easy-to-sew product. Have a supply of ¾"-wide Velcro strips on hand because many projects will need this closure. The two halves of the Velcro strips are described as the hook/rough side and the loop/soft side. For some projects, the ¾" strips will be cut in half horizontally for narrow strips. (Fig. 2)

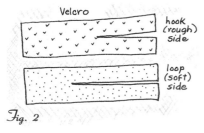

Fig. 2

Use a **Teflon presser foot** when sewing projects in vinyl or oilcloth. The bottom surface of the foot glides along these fabrics and does not stick. Check your sewing machine accessory box for a Teflon foot or purchase one at your local sewing machine store or mail order sewing supplier. (See the Resource listing on page 128.)

Be sure the **sewing machine needle** is correctly sized for the project you sew. Thick fabrics require a needle sized 100 or 110. Jeans needles are also good choices for sewing on layers of denim. You'll be rewarded for using the right needles by less needle breakage.

Ultrasuede (or **Sensuede**) is a manufactured suede-like fabric that does not fray and is available in beautiful colors. For the projects in this book, small pieces and strips are useful for zipper grabber tabs, zipper pulls, and reinforcing pieces. The fabric is easy to work with and machine washable and dryable. (See the Resource listing on page 128.)

When it's time to draw lines or marks on fabric, have **chalk markers** or **wash-away markers** on hand. I also like to save and use soap bar slivers for making easy-to-remove marks on fabrics.

▪▪ TIMELY TECHNIQUES

Make Your Own Handles and Straps

Many projects suggest using webbing for handles and straps. Webbing can be purchased by the yard at fabric and craft stores. It can save time since it's ready to sew when you cut it to the length you need.

You may prefer to make your own handles and straps if you want the strap color to match the bag or if you don't have webbing on hand. Start with 3"-wide strips of fabric cut to the required length of the handle. On one long edge of the fabric, turn under ¼" to the wrong side of the fabric and press the edge in place. (Fig. 3)

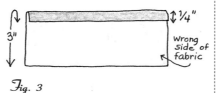

Fig. 3

On the opposite edge, measure and press under 1". (Fig. 4)

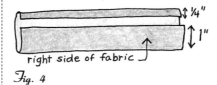

Fig. 4

Bring the ¼" folded edge over the raw edge of the 1" fold and press. Sew one or two seams on the edge of the top fold and your handle is completed. (Fig. 5)

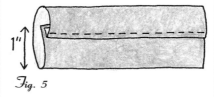

Fig. 5

Make Box Corners on Tote Bags

It's easy to change the bottom of a flat bag into a bag with bottom corners and dimension. (Fig. 6)

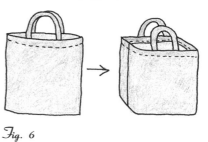

Fig. 6

With the bag inside out, fold the side seamline to meet the bottom seamline and pin. (Fig. 7)

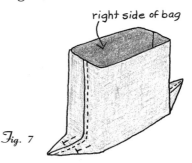

Fig. 7

Measure and mark a line across the folded triangular area and sew across on the line. It's always a good idea to sew twice or reinforce the stitching so the bottom seam of the bag is strong. (Fig. 8)

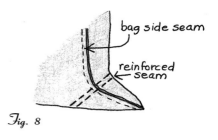

Fig. 8

Make a Double Drawstring

Two drawstrings in a casing make a fast way to close the top of a bag. To add a double drawstring, you'll need two openings in the casing. (Fig. 9)

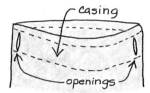

Fig. 9

Cut two pieces of cord or ribbon the length of the entire casing. Thread cord #1 into opening #1, all around the casing, past the second opening, and out through opening #1. (Fig. 10)

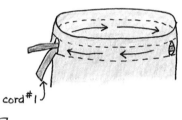

cord #1

Fig. 10

Thread cord #2 into the second opening, all around the casing, and back out through opening #2. (Fig. 11)

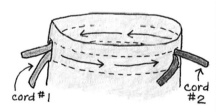

cord #1   cord #2

Fig. 11

Knot the ends of each pair of cords together and pull on them at the same time to draw the top of the bag closed. (Fig. 12)

Fig. 12

Add Grabber Tabs to Zippers

From studying purchased bags, I discovered the value of adding tabs to the ends of zippers. (Fig. 13) They make it easier to open and close the zippers because there's something to grab and hold while the other hand pulls on the zipper head.

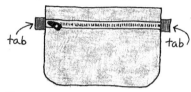

tab   tab

Fig. 13

Grabber tabs can be made from a folded piece of ribbon or tape, a square of Ultrasuede, or a piece of cord. (Fig. 14)

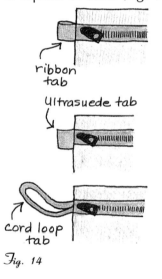

ribbon tab

Ultrasuede tab

cord loop tab

Fig. 14

Pin the tabs over the zipper ends before sewing a piece of fabric over the zipper. (Fig. 15) It's always a good idea to sew back and forth over the tab and zipper end area to make sure the tab is firmly attached.

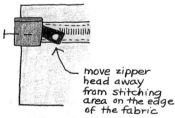

move zipper head away from stitching area on the edge of the fabric

Fig. 15

Add Pull Ties to Zipper Heads

A zipper is always easier to open and close if it has an additional pull tie to grab. (Fig. 16) This feature helps everyone, including those who have hand coordination problems or arthritis.

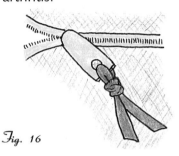

Fig. 16

If you are using standard clothing zippers, the opening in the zipper head is small. Cut the ribbon or fabric strip at an angle to make it easier to thread it into the opening. Here are two tying options for pull ties. (Fig. 17)

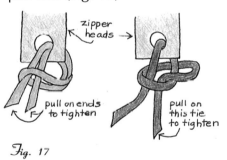

zipper heads

pull on ends to tighten   pull on this tie to tighten

Fig. 17

Travel Hint
I found this applique design of a man and his suitcase on a vintage towel in an antique shop. He's a symbol with the travel hints scattered throughout this book. The towel is a great addition to my old linens collection and a souvenir of a memorable trip.

The first travel hint: Support your local travel agent for a valuable and time-saving source of information and assistance.

The World's Easiest Zipper Method
(The Exposed Zipper)

There's no fear with sewing the exposed zipper — it really is easy.

1. Start with a zipper longer than the piece of fabric to which it will be sewn. The zipper can be either slightly longer or much longer, since any excess length will be cut off. (Fig. 1)

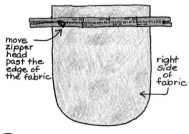

Fig. 1

Make sure the zipper is flat and has no creases in it from being packaged. It's much easier to work with the zipper by pressing it flat now.

2. Place and pin the zipper 1" below the top edge of the right side of the fabric. (Fig. 2)

move zipper head past the edge of the fabric

right side of fabric

Fig. 2

3. Sew around all four sides of the zipper. You can use the special zipper presser foot if you prefer, or use a standard presser foot. You can also move the needle position on the machine

to sew closer to the left side of the presser foot and closer to the zipper teeth. (Fig. 3)

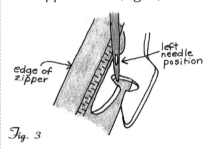

edge of zipper

left needle position

Fig. 3

Sew twice around the zipper for the most secure hold, especially for fabrics that fray easily. Move the zipper head inside the stitching line. (Fig. 4)

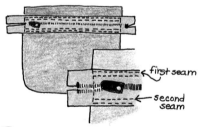

first seam

second seam

Fig. 4

4. Cut off the extra length of zipper that extends beyond the stitching lines. Then cut the fabric from the back of the zipper teeth. (Fig. 5)

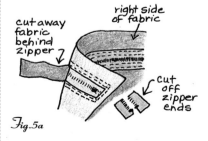

right side of fabric

cut away fabric behind zipper

cut off zipper ends

Fig. 5a

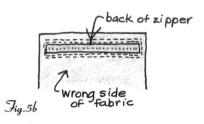

back of zipper

wrong side of fabric

Fig. 5b

That's all it takes!

After sewing the zipper to the right side of the fabric, cut away the fabric behind the zipper on the back side.

Sew decorative trim over the edges of the zipper tape if you want to cover more of the zipper. You'll see examples of this on several projects in the book: the "Anything" Bags on page 11, the Backpack Purse on page 57, and the Car Kit bag on page 110.

"Anything" Bags and Pockets

An assortment of "Anything" Bags. Use the exposed zipper method on fabrics of any type, size, and shape to make these handy storage bags. The lace fabric bag at the upper left (pink zipper) is used as a mesh laundry bag. Note the zipper grabber tabs on many of the bags and the zipper pulls. The silver hammered pull is a spinner from a fishing lure! Use your imagination for other ideas for zipper pulls.

USE THE WORLD'S EASIEST ZIPPER METHOD TO MAKE THE WORLD'S EASIEST BAGS AND POCKETS. I CALL THEM "ANYTHING" BAGS AND POCKETS BECAUSE YOU CAN STORE ANYTHING IN THEM. MAKE THEM IN FABRICS, SIZES, AND SHAPES OF YOUR CHOICE.

1. Follow the instructions on page 10 for sewing an exposed zipper to a piece of fabric. Cut another piece of fabric the same size. (Fig. 1)

Fig. 1

2. Open the zipper a short distance to make it easier to turn the bag right side out. Pin the two pieces of fabric with right sides together. If you want to add zipper grabber tabs (see page 9), pin them at the ends of the zipper and between the two fabric pieces. (Fig. 2)

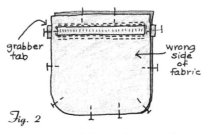

Fig. 2

Sew around the edges with ¼" seam allowances, clip the corners, and trim the seam allowances. (Fig. 3)

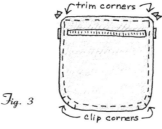

Fig. 3

3. Turn the bag right side out through the zipper opening. Press the edges and tie a zipper pull to the head of the zipper (see page 9). You've finished!

4. An **"Anything" Pocket** is a single piece of fabric with the zipper sewn in place. All you have to do is turn under and press all four sides of the fabric. (Fig. 4)

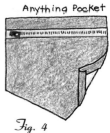

Fig. 4

5. Pin the pocket inside or outside on a tote bag, a garment, or anywhere you want a protected storage space. Sew around the edges and add a pull tie to the zipper head. Zipper grabber tabs can also be added to the zipper ends on a pocket. (Fig. 5)

Fig. 5

Simple Stuff Sacks

Simple Stuff Sacks can be used for everyday storage for gifts, for laundry, and for holding stuffed animals.

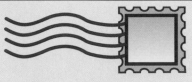

To all my friends

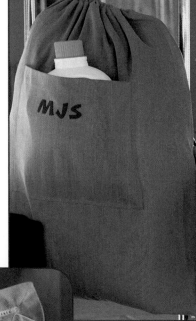

Circle Bags and Duffel Bags

Sew Circle Bags from a variety of fabrics and make them in many sizes. Use fabrics left over from a quilting project to piece a Circle Bag as seen on the left front. Denim trimmed with decorative yarns was selected from a sewing experiment for the bag in the center. Light green and pink Sandcastle fabrics by Dan River.

CIRCLES ON THE ENDS FORM THE SHAPE OF THESE BAGS. USE THE PATTERNS INCLUDED IN THE BOOK (PAGE 118) OR MAKE PATTERNS IN OTHER SIZES. TO DETERMINE THE SIZE OF THE FABRIC NEEDED FOR DIFFERENT CIRCLES, MEASURE AROUND THE CIRCLE WITH A TAPE MEASURE ON ITS EDGE. FABRICS FOR THESE BAGS INCLUDE MEDIUM TO HEAVYWEIGHT FABRICS SUCH AS DENIM, TAPESTRY, POLARFLEECE, CORDUROY, TERRYCLOTH, QUILTED FABRICS, AND ULTRASUEDE.

Basic Circle Bag

MAKE A CIRCLE BAG TO HOLD COSMETICS OR TOILETRIES, A WEEK'S SUPPLY OF
UNDERWEAR, OR A CHINA CUP, TEA BAGS, AND SUPPLIES FOR A TEA PARTY IN A
HOTEL ROOM.

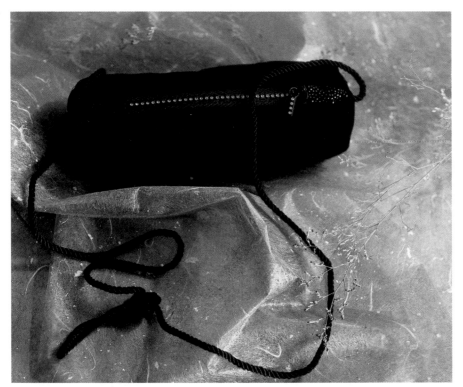

*Use the dimensions for the small Circle Bag and adapt the project for an
evening bag. Select black quilted velvet, a rhinestone trimmed zipper, and
satin cord to make this simple bag perfect for an elegant event.*

Supplies:

½ yd. medium to heavyweight fabric
Zipper:
     9" for small bag
     14" for medium bag
     16" for large bag
4" piece of ribbon for end tabs (optional)

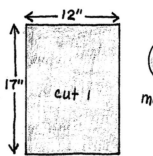

Fig. 1

Steps:

1. Trace the appropriate size Circle Bag pattern
from page 118 and cut two from fabric. Cut
one piece of fabric 9" square for the small bag,
12" x 17" for the medium bag, or 14" x 20"
for the large bag. (Fig. 1)

2. Sew the zipper to the edges of the bag (9"
edges for small, 12" edges for medium, or 14"
edges for large). Either turn under the edges
¼", press, and sew the zipper to the folded-
under edges, or sew the zipper to the right side
of the fabric so it's exposed. (Fig. 2)

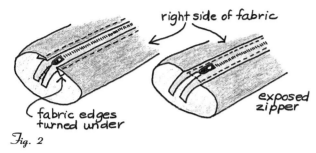

right side of fabric

exposed zipper

fabric edges turned under

Fig. 2

3. Fold the circle ends in quarters and mark the folds. Also mark the quarter sections on the edges of both ends of the bag fabric. (Fig. 3)

Fig. 3

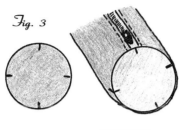

4. Pin a 2" piece of folded ribbon or a small piece of Ultrasuede to each end of the zipper. (Fig. 4)

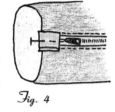

Fig. 4

5. Match up and pin the quarter marks on the circles and bag ends with the right sides of the fabric together. Open the zipper a short distance. Slowly sew the circle ends to the bag,

reinforcing the stitching across the zipper and tabs. (Fig. 5) Turn the bag right side out through the zipper opening.

wrong side of fabric

zipper partially open

Fig. 5

6. If you experiment with different circle and bag sizes, you may discover that the circle is smaller than the width of the end of the bag. Instead of re-sewing the zipper, make it easy for yourself by slightly gathering the bag fabric to fit the circle. (Fig. 6)

Fig. 6

Option: Sew an "Anything" Pocket (see page 11) inside or outside the bag for extra storage, as illustrated in Fig. 6.

Duffel Bag

THIS CIRCLE BAG IS AN EXTRA-LARGE SIZE. USE IT AS A CARRY-ON BAG FOR AN AIRPLANE FLIGHT, AS A TEEN'S SPORT BAG, OR FOR TRIPS TO THE SPA OR GYM. CHOOSE STURDY FABRIC FOR THIS BAG.

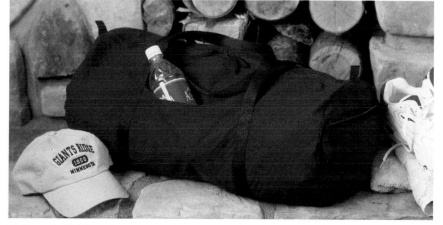

Make a duffel bag for trips to the gym and fitness center. The circle end of the bag features a zipper pocket for extra storage. Sandcastle fabric by Dan River.

Steps:

1. Trace the Duffel Bag Circle pattern from page 119. Cut two circles from fabric and two from lining fabric if you plan to line the bag ends or make pockets. Cut one piece of fabric 25" x 33" and a front pocket piece 12" x 26". (Fig. 1)

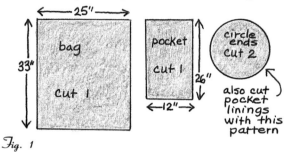

Fig. 1

2. On the 12" ends of the front pocket fabric, zigzag or serge the edges and fold back and sew a 1" hem to the wrong sides of the fabric. (Fig. 2) Add a monogram or other trim to the right side at this time.

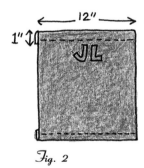

Fig. 2

3. Center and pin the pocket on the right side of the bag fabric so the center horizontal and vertical lines of both the pocket and bag line up. (Measure or fold to find the centers.) Draw and sew across two lines 2" from the center of the pocket pieces. These lines form the bottoms of each pocket. (Fig. 3)

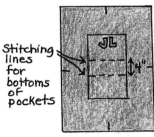

Stitching lines for bottoms of pockets

Fig. 3

4. Pin and sew the handles to the bag. Fold the webbing in quarters and mark each fold with a pin. Begin by pinning one end over the outer pocket edge at the bottom center line of the bag. Pin the handle to the side edge of the pocket. The first quarter marker pin will be the top of the handle loop. (Fig. 4)

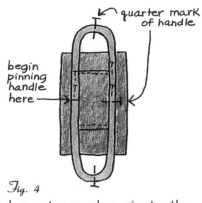

quarter mark of handle

begin pinning handle here

Fig. 4

Pin the second quarter marker pin to the center of the pocket edge and continue to pin along the pocket edge. The third marker pin will be the top of the second handle loop.

5. Sew the zipper or zippers to the 25" ends of the bag fabric. If using two zippers, pin them to the edges of the fabric with the zipper heads meeting in the center. (Fig. 5) Sew the zippers to the bag.

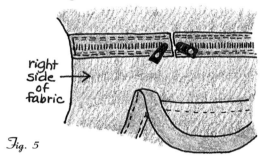

right side of fabric

Fig. 5

6. To make the pocket on the circle ends of the bag, sew a zipper 2½" down from the top center point of the circle end, using the exposed method (see page 10). Sew the pocket lining, right side down, to the wrong side of the circle. (Fig. 6)

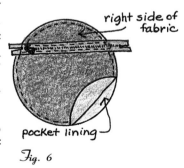

right side of fabric

pocket lining

Fig. 6

7. Fold and mark the quarter sections on both the bag circle ends and the bag fabric. Pin and sew the circles to the bag by matching the marks and with the right sides of the fabric together. Add another row of stitching to strengthen the bag and zigzag or serge the circle edges.

8. Turn the bag right side out and tie zipper pulls (see page 9) to the ends of all three zippers.

Circle Bag Variations

Simple Round Bag

1. To make this bag, use the extra-large Circle Bag pattern on page 118 and cut two circles from fabric. Also cut two 12" x 3" strips of fabric for the side section.

right side of fabric

Fig. 1

2. Use a 12" or longer zipper. Sew the zipper in the center of one 12" strip and sew the second strip to the ends of the zipper to form a circle. (Fig. 1)

3. Pin and sew the two fabric circles to the circular strip.

The Simple Round Bag becomes an entertainment storage bag trimmed with rows of buttons for a monogram. Sandcastle quilted fabric by Dan River,

4. To add a button outline monogram, draw a letter or letters on the bag with a wash-away or chalk marker. Sew buttons along the lines.

Neck Roll Pillow

Stuff a long circle bag with plastic bags or fiberfill for a comfortable neck roll pillow for plane or car trips. Sandcastle quilted fabric by Dan River.

1. Use the small Circle Bag pattern on page 118 and cut two circles. Cut a 9" x 16" piece of fabric. (Fig. 1)

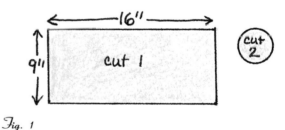

16"

9"

cut 1

cut 2

Fig. 1

2. Sew the bag together using Steps 1 through 5 of the instructions for the Basic Circle Bag.

To use this bag as a neck pillow, you can stuff it with fiberfill, using less stuffing in the center so the bag will wrap around your neck. For a compact way to carry the bag with you, bring along the empty bag and two plastic dry cleaner bags. Fold up the plastic bags into a small compact square and hold them together, along with the folded pillow, with rubber bands. When you're ready to use the neck roll pillow, unwrap the plastic bags and stuff them into the pillow.

Wave Top Bag

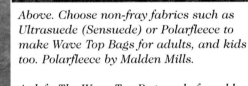

Above. Choose non-fray fabrics such as Ultrasuede (Sensuede) or Polarfleece to make Wave Top Bags for adults, and kids too. Polarfleece by Malden Mills.

At left. The Wave Top Bag made from black Ultrasuede (Sensuede) and a double drawstring of shiny satin cord makes a perfect special occasion handbag. Satin cord by Wrights.

YOU'LL FIND LOTS OF USES FOR THIS BAG WITH THE UNUSUAL WAVY TOP EDGE. WHEN YOU PULL THE BAG DRAWSTRING TO CLOSE IT, THE TOP CLOSES TIGHTLY WITH NO BULK OR RUFFLES. I CARRY A HAIR DRYER IN A POLARFLEECE VERSION OF THIS BAG AND MY YOUNG NEPHEW STORES SMALL STUFFED ANIMALS IN THE BAG I SEWED FOR HIM. CHOOSE SOFT FABRIC THAT DOESN'T RAVEL SUCH AS ULTRASUEDE, POLARFLEECE, FELT, OR LEATHER.

Supplies:

⅓ yd. non-fraying fabric
24" of cording
Cord lock
Buttonhole or eyelet cutter, or razor blade
  for cutting holes for cord

Steps:

1. Trace the Wave Top Bag pattern and all the markings on the pattern from page 117 and cut four from fabric. (Fig. 1) If you have chosen to work with Polarfleece, cut no more than two pieces at a time due to the bulk of the fabric. For an interesting top edge for this bag, cut the wavy edges with pinking shears.

Fig. 1

2. Pin one side of two bag pieces together with right sides facing. Sew two edges together using a ¼" seam allowance and reinforcing the stitching at the top edge. (Fig. 2)

Pin and sew the second set of pieces together in the same way. Then sew the two sets together, with the right sides of the fabric together. (Fig. 3)

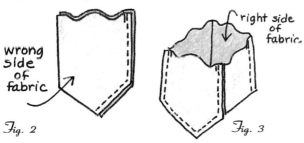

wrong side of fabric

right side of fabric

Fig. 2   *Fig. 3*

3. Trim and clip the seam allowances and turn the bag right side out.

4. Slide a piece of thick cardboard or a cutting board inside the top edge of the bag. Use the paper pattern markings to make cuts or holes on all four sides of the bag. (Fig. 4)

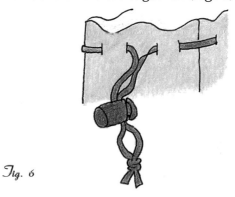

cardboard

Fig. 4

5. Thread the cord through the holes with a bodkin or safety pin, beginning with the right

center hole in the side you want as the bag front and bringing the cord all the way around the bag. (Fig. 5)

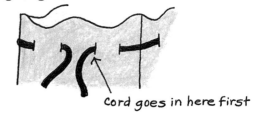

Fig. 5   Cord goes in here first

Slide the cord lock over the two ends of the cord and tie knots at the end of each cord, or knot the two ends together. (Fig. 6)

Fig. 6

Hint: If you are using cording that ravels easily, tightly wrap the ends with cellophane tape. This will make it easier to thread the cord through the holes or cuts in the fabric. To make sure the knots at the ends stay tied, add a drop or two of clear-drying glue.

6. The wave top bag is complete and ready to be stuffed for your next trip. (Fig. 7)

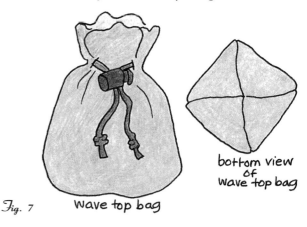

Fig. 7   wave top bag

bottom view of wave top bag

Option: An elegant black fabric version stores pantyhose in the suitcase, then becomes an evening bag for a special occasion.

Stuff Sacks

Sew Easy

Stuff sacks are perfect for camping, kayaking, and everyday storage. The variegated nylon sack features a zipper sewn into the sack's side seam. In the center, a towel and water bottle are stored in a stuff sack made of nylon bug screen, and the gray print sack on the right features an exposed zipper for easy side access to the contents of the bag. Fabrics, cord, and cord locks from The RainShed.

THESE ALL-PURPOSE STORAGE BAGS ARE PERFECT FOR CAMPING, EVERYDAY TRIPS, OR HAULING SPORTS GEAR. USE THE BAG DIMENSIONS PROVIDED OR PLAN BAG SIZES TO FIT YOUR SPECIAL NEEDS. FABRIC CHOICES INCLUDE MESH, POLARFLEECE, NYLON, COTTON, ULTRASUEDE, FLANNEL, TERRYCLOTH, OR OTHER FABRICS SOFT ENOUGH SO THE TOP OF THE BAG CAN BE PULLED TOGETHER WITH A DRAWSTRING.

Steps:

1. Trace the Stuff Sack Bottom Circle pattern from page 127 and cut one from fabric. Cut a piece of fabric 13" x 16". (Fig. 1)

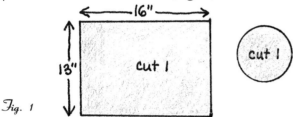

Fig. 1

2. Pin together the two 13" edges of the fabric with the right side of the fabric inside. Sew down 1" from the top edge and reinforce the stitching. Leave a 1" opening and then continue sewing down the bag edges. (Fig. 2)

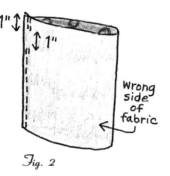

Fig. 2

3. Mark quarter folds on both the circle end and the bottom of the bag. (Fig. 3)

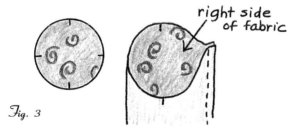

Fig. 3

Match and pin the marks with the right side of the circle facing the right side of the bag, and sew the circle to the bag with a ¼" seam allowance. (Fig. 4)

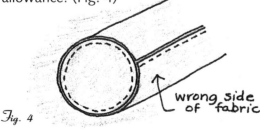

Fig. 4

4. Keeping the bag wrong side out, zigzag stitch around the top edge. Then turn over and fold 1" of the top edge so the right side of the fabric shows. (Fig. 5) Sew the edge to the bag and turn the bag right side out.

Fig. 5

5. Use a bodkin or safety pin to insert the cord through the seamline opening and around the casing back to the opening. Slide a cord lock over the cord ends and knot the ends of the cord.

Options:

- To make a Stuff Sack with a zipper down the side of the bag, sew the zipper to the side edges of the bag fabric. The top edges of the zipper will be 2" below the top edges of the fabric. (Fig. 6)

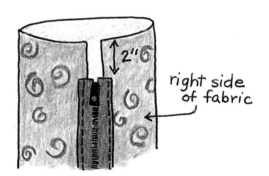

Fig. 6

- After sewing in the zipper, continue assembling the bag from Step 3 above. This feature allows access to the contents of the bag while it is hanging on a peg on the wall or in a tent.

- Make a Stuff Sack to store a rolled-up sleeping bag. The approximate dimensions for this bag would be a 10" diameter circle for the bottom, and a piece of fabric 31" wide and 20" long. However, it's best to measure the actual rolled-up sleeping bag to test these measurements.

First Class Laundry Bag

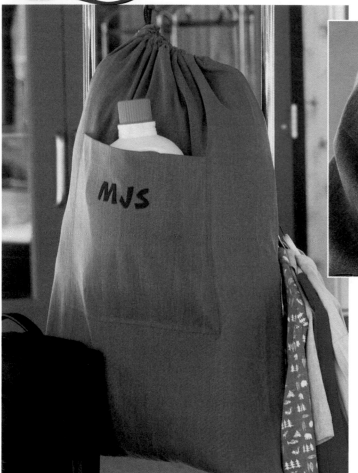

Above. A small hidden pocket inside the outer pocket of the First Class Laundry Bag holds a supply of money for coin-operated washers and dryers.

At left. A practical addition to any laundry bag is a large front pocket for carrying a bottle of laundry soap. A monogram personalizes the bag, a perfect gift for a student moving to college. Denim fabric from The RainShed.

ORDINARY LAUNDRY BAGS ARE EASY TO FIND, BUT THIS VERSION TAKES DIRTY CLOTHES TO A HIGHER LEVEL! A LARGE FRONT POCKET HOLDS A BOTTLE OF LAUNDRY SOAP AND INSIDE THE POCKET IS A SMALLER ONE WITH A ZIPPER TO STORE THE COINS NEEDED FOR WASHING AND DRYING CLOTHES. MAKE THIS BAG FOR HIGH SCHOOL GRADUATES WHO ARE LEAVING HOME FOR COLLEGE. THIS IS A VERY DOWN-TO-EARTH GIFT BUT ONE THAT WILL BE APPRECIATED BY THE STUDENT WHEN HE OR SHE MAKES A TRIP TO THE LAUNDRY ROOM. FABRICS TO CONSIDER ARE DENIM, CANVAS, HEAVY GRADE NYLON, AND OTHER VERY STURDY FABRICS. I ALSO RECOMMEND A DARK COLOR.

Supplies:

1 yd. 60"-wide or 1½ yds. 45"-wide
   sturdy fabric
1½ yd. cord

Cord lock
Zipper, 7" for hidden coin pocket
Small piece of Ultrasuede or other fabric
   for monogram
Small piece of paper-backed fusible web

Steps:

1. Cut three pieces of fabric: a 36" x 45" piece for the bag, a 15" square for the large pocket, and a 6" square for the coin pocket. (Fig. 1)

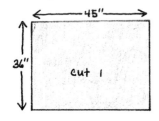
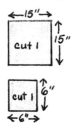

Fig. 1

2. Sew the zipper to the 6" square, placing the zipper 1" below the top edge of the fabric. Use the exposed zipper method on page 10. Turn under all four edges of the fabric ¼" and press. (Fig. 2) Set the pocket aside.

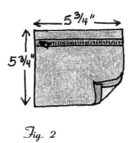

Fig. 2

3. Zigzag on the top edge of the 15" square large pocket. Fold under and press 1½" from this edge to the wrong side of the pocket. Sew the hem to the pocket. Turn under the other three raw edges ½" and press. (Fig. 3)

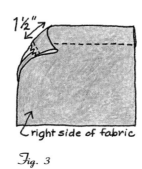

right side of fabric

Fig. 3

4. Use the letters from the alphabet on page 116 to monogram the pocket. Trace the letters on the paper side of paper-backed fusible web. Following the directions that come with the product, fuse the letters to the wrong side of the monogram fabric. Cut out the letters and peel the paper off the back. Position the letters near the top of the pocket and fuse them in place. (If you are using Ultrasuede, remember to cover the letters with a press cloth so the surface of the iron doesn't imprint a design on them.)

5. Position the large pocket on the laundry bag front. Center it on half of the long edge of the fabric, 12" from the top edge. (Fig. 4)

Pin the pocket in place on the bottom edge only and mark a line on the bag where the top edge of the pocket will fall. Pin and sew the coin pocket 2" below the line on the bag and inside the large pocket. Sew around all edges of

the coin pocket to attach it to the bag. (Fig. 5)

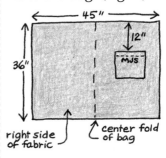

right side of fabric · center fold of bag

Fig. 4

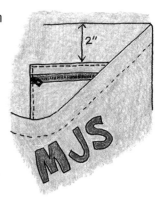

Fig. 5

Pin the large pocket in place and sew two seams ¼" apart to securely attach this pocket that will hold heavy bottles of laundry soap. (Fig. 6)

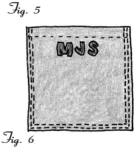

Fig. 6

6. Fold the bag in half along the long edge with wrong sides out. Sew along the side edge 2½" down from the top edge and reinforce the stitching. Leave a 1" opening and reinforce the stitching again as you sew the rest of the side and bottom seams to create the bag. (Fig. 7)

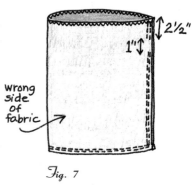

wrong side of fabric

Fig. 7

7. Zigzag stitch or serge the top edge of the bag. Fold and pin the edge 2" to the wrong side of the bag and sew twice around to secure the edge. For extra strength at the opening, I stitched a small triangle of Ultrasuede where this seam and the side seam intersect. (Fig. 8)

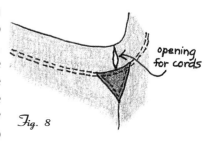

opening for cords

Fig. 8

8. Turn the bag right side out and use a bodkin or safety pin to insert the drawstring. Add a cord lock to conveniently pull and hold the bag closed.

Option: Make a double drawstring closure for this bag (page 8) and eliminate the need for a cord lock.

Jeans-Leg Bag

Sew Easy

Recycle the legs of old jeans by turning them into clever storage bags. Belt loops form the casing for the drawstring ties and a jeans pocket trims one bag, adding another storage place.

SALVAGE A LEG OF AN OLD PAIR OF JEANS TO MAKE THIS UNIQUE STUFF BAG. THE JEANS BELT LOOPS HOLD THE CORD TIE IN PLACE AND A JEANS POCKET ADDS EXTRA TRIM. MAKE THIS BAG FOR KIDS OR TEENS OR AS A GIFT BAG FOR A BOTTLE OF HERB VINEGAR OR WINE. CONSIDER THAT LEGS FROM CHILDREN'S JEANS MAKE SMALLER BAGS THAN LEGS OF ADULT SIZE JEANS. THIS IS ONE WAY TO COMMEMORATE AND RECYCLE A SPECIAL PAIR OF JEANS.

Supplies:

Pair of old jeans
24" length of cording
Cord lock (optional)
Size 90 or 100 needle or a jeans sewing
    machine needle

Steps:

1. Cut four or five belt loops from the jeans. Instead of trying to remove the bar tack stitching holding the loops in place, cut around the stitching and trim away the jeans fabric behind the loops. (Fig. 1)

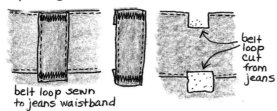

belt loop sewn
to jeans waistband

belt
loop
cut
from
jeans

Fig. 1

2. Cut 20" (or any length you prefer) from the bottom edge of the leg. You can use either the hem end of the leg or the cut end of the leg as the bag top. (Fig. 2) If the cut end of the leg will be the top, trim off the hem at the bottom edge.

bag top

cut off jeans
hem for this
bag

Fig. 2

3. If you want to sew a jeans pocket to the bag, do it now. Trim the pocket from the jeans in the same way you cut off the belt loops, cutting away the jeans from the sides and inside of the pocket. Place the pocket approximately 5" from the bottom edge of the bag and stitch around the outer edges. (Fig. 3)

5"

Fig. 3

4. Turn the leg inside out. At the bottom of the bag, bring the two leg seams together, placing the bulk of the seam allowances to either side of the meeting point. (Fig. 4) Pin together.

Fold in the edges of the denim to the center, as illustrated. (Fig. 5)

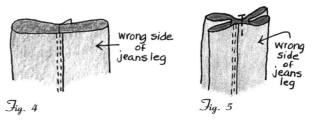

wrong side
of
jeans leg

wrong
side
of
jeans
leg

Fig. 4   *Fig. 5*

Pin the folds in place and sew twice across the bottom edge, sewing slowly through the layers of denim. Turn the leg right side out. The bottom of the bag is shaped by the folds and the stitching that holds them in place.

5. Decide how far from the top edge you will place the belt loops. Remember that the cord will shift to the top edge of the loops when pulled tight. Pin the belt loops to the bag, spacing them an equal distance apart. Sew slowly across each end of each loop, sewing inside the bar tacking. (Fig. 6)

Sew to
attach
belt loop

Fig. 6

Thread the cord through the loops and add a cord lock or tie and knot the cord ends to close the bag.

6. Cut the top edge of the bag with pinking shears, or turn the hem under and sew. Sew carefully over thick seam areas.

Option: Sew a casing on the top of the bag and add a double drawstring, as described on page 8.

Travel Hint

In foreign countries, shop at food stores for souvenirs and gifts for your friends and relatives at home. You'll find interesting and inexpensive items in cans and jars labeled in foreign languages.

Easy Napkin Petal Pouch

Sew Easy

Dinner napkins and handkerchiefs become Easy Napkin Petal Pouches with minimal sewing required.

WHY MAKE AN ORDINARY DRAWSTRING BAG WHEN YOU CAN MAKE THIS VERSION SO QUICKLY? CHOOSE A DINNER NAPKIN, A HANDKERCHIEF, OR A SQUARE OF FABRIC TO MAKE A POUCH PERFECT FOR A GIFT OR FOR CARRYING LOTION AND TREATS FOR A SPA NIGHT AWAY FROM HOME. A SOLID COLOR NAPKIN WORKS WELL SINCE BOTH SIDES OF THE FABRIC SHOW. FOR THE BEST RESULTS, SELECT SOFT, THIN FABRICS. POLARFLEECE DOESN'T WORK WELL FOR THIS PROJECT BECAUSE IT IS TOO THICK AND WON'T GATHER TIGHTLY IN THE CENTER.

Supplies:

18" square napkin, handkerchief, or fabric piece
4 yd. cord or ribbon

Steps:

1. Place the napkin flat on a table and turn back and pin the four corners so the points measure 5" to the fold. (Fig. 1)

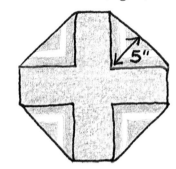

Fig. 1

2. Sew 1"-wide casings through each folded corner, reinforcing the stitching on the edges. (Fig. 2)

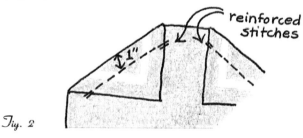

reinforced stitches

Fig. 2

3. Cut the cord in two 2-yard pieces and thread one through the casings, starting and ending the first cord in the same opening. Thread the second cord through the opening on the opposite side of the napkin. Knot the ends of each cord together. (Fig. 3)

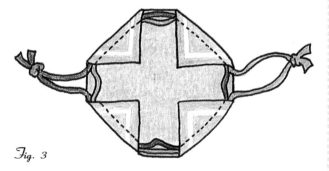

Fig. 3

4. Pull the cords to gather the napkin into a pouch. Pull out the napkin corners to make them appear as petals.

5. For the handkerchief size pouch, fold in the corners to measure 3½". Sew ½"-wide casings. Measure around the edges of the handkerchief and cut two cords to that measurement. Follow Steps 3 and 4 above to complete the pouch.

Options:

- The long cords on this pouch can be cut shorter if it is not important that the bag be opened flat.
- Choose elegant evening wear fabrics to make a purse.
- See the Comfort Kit on page 108 for another use for this pouch.

Travel Hint

Experienced travelers learn to carry items that make life more comfortable away from home. The list of important things to pack varies for each person. Mine includes a shawl (pareu rolled up and held with rubber bands), a heating pad with an extension cord, a clothespin to hold window draperies closed, lavender bath oil, herb tea bags, a flat rubber sink stopper, dental floss for use on teeth and tying things together, a Swiss Army knife (in checked luggage), and socks to keep my feet warm. What are your essentials? Make your list below.

_____

_____

_____

_____

_____

_____

_____

_____

_____

_____

_____

Smart Storage Bags

Smart Storage Bags are practical projects to hold essential travel supplies. Give them as gifts and you'll hear compliments!

To all my friends

Shoe Bag

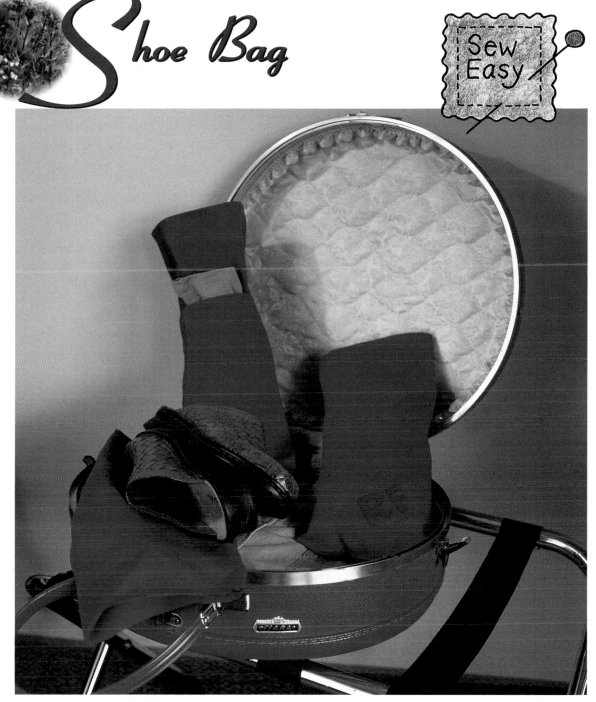

An extra storage pocket for stockings or pantyhose and a monogram are two ways to personalize shoe bags made from knit stretch fabrics. Turn under the top open edges and hem the bags or simply cut the top edges with pinking shears, as shown on the royal blue bag on the left. Fabrics from The RainShed.

*S*EW THIS QUICK-TO-MAKE BAG FROM KNIT FABRIC THAT STRETCHES TO HOLD A PAIR OF SHOES. FOR AN EXTRA FEATURE, ADD A POCKET TO STORE PANTYHOSE OR SHOE CARE ITEMS. USING THIS BAG IN YOUR SUITCASE WILL PROTECT THE CLOTHING AND KEEP THE SUITCASE CLEAN. I USED LYCRA STRETCH KNITS, BUT STANDARD KNITS OR RIBBING WORK WELL ALSO.

Supplies:

½ yd. knit fabric

Steps:

1. For a pair of women's shoes, cut a piece of fabric 14" x 16". For men's shoes, cut the fabric 17" x 18". (Fig. 1)

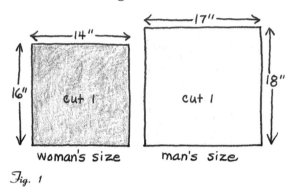

Fig. 1

For shoes with thick soles, measure around the pair to make a bag that fits. (Fig. 2)

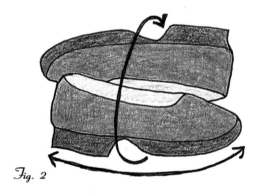

Fig. 2

2. On the top edge (14" for women, 17" for men), turn under ¼", press, and sew. For a quicker edge finish, trim the top edge with pinking shears. Proceed to Step 5 if you do not plan to sew an extra pocket on the shoe bag.

3. To add the outside pocket, cut another piece of knit fabric half the bag width (7" for women, 8½" for men) and 11" long. On the top (shorter) edge of the pocket, turn under ¼", press, and sew.

4. Mark the vertical center line of the bag. Place and pin the pocket (right sides of fabric together) between the center line and one side edge of the bag. Sew the pocket to the bag on the center line. (Fig. 3)

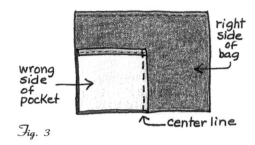

Fig. 3

Turn the pocket over so the right side of the fabric is up. Pin the pocket edges to the bag. (Fig. 4)

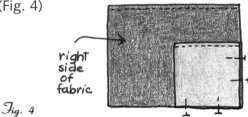

Fig. 4

5. Fold the bag in half vertically, with right sides together. Sew around the bottom and sides of the bag. Clip the fabric at the corners and trim the seam allowance. (Fig. 5)

Turn the bag right side out and stuff it with a pair of shoes. (Fig. 6)

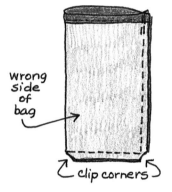

Fig. 5

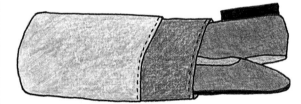

Fig. 6

Option: Personalize a shoe bag by machine stitching the owner's name across the top of the bag.

I refer to this shoe bag as the "Barbara Bush Shoe Bag." After watching a television interview and learning that she wears mismatched tennis shoes, I assumed she used shoe bags that held only one shoe and then she got distracted while packing. Not so. She deliberately wears them that way. For others who prefer to wear two of the same shoe, it makes sense to keep both shoes in the same bag.

Drawstring Jewelry Bag

Separate and store jewelry pieces in the see-through pockets of the Drawstring Jewelry Bag. Add a circle of plastic needlepoint canvas for holding and supporting pierced earrings or pins. Also see the pink-lined bag on the book's front cover. Pink and teal fabrics by Marcus Brothers Textiles.

Store jewelry inside this compact bag with its eight individual pockets. Add a circle of plastic needlepoint canvas for holding and supporting pierced earrings or pins. The see-through fabric of the inside circle allows you to see and identify the jewelry quickly. Make this bag as a gift to a high school graduate or a favorite babysitter. You're sure to receive many compliments. Fabrics to use for this bag include cotton, linen, silk, and other thin, soft fabrics.

Supplies:

- ½ yd. cotton fabric (I used two different fabrics for the outside and inside circles)
- ⅓ yd. mesh fabric or bridal tulle for inside storage circle
- 1 yd. bias tape for binding inside circle
- 1 yd. cord
- Cord lock
- 4" circle of plastic needlepoint canvas (optional)

Steps:

1. Trace the Drawstring Jewelry Bag patterns from page 120. The patterns show only ¼ of each circle. Make a full size pattern for each circle by placing the patterns on paper that is folded in quarters. Cut two large circles from cotton fabrics and cut one smaller inside circle from mesh fabric, or two layers of bridal tulle. (Fig. 1)

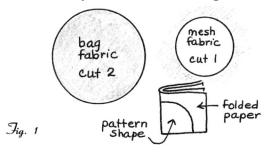

Fig. 1

2. With the right sides of the large fabric circles together, sew around the entire edge with a ¼" seam allowance. Trim and clip the seam allowance or trim with pinking shears. Make a 1" cut in the center of the fabric that will be inside the bag and turn the fabrics right side out through the cut. (Fig. 2)

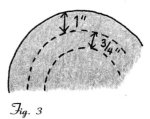

Fig. 2

3. To create a drawstring casing in the fabric circles, sew a circle 1" from the outer edge. Then sew another circle ¾" farther in from the first stitching line. (Fig. 3)

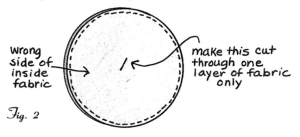

Fig. 3

4. Sew bias tape to the edge of the mesh fabric circle. Center and pin the mesh circle on the inside bag circle. Trace a 3" diameter circle in the center of the mesh circle, using the pattern traced from the book. Then draw eight straight lines (spokes) from the center circle to the edges of the mesh circle. Sew around the 3" circle and on all the lines. These lines will form the pocket divisions in the mesh circle. (Fig. 4)

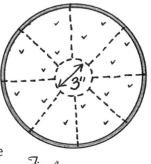

Fig. 4

5. Carefully cut an opening in the drawstring casing through the outer fabric only. (Fig. 5)

Fig. 5

Use a large safety pin or bodkin to thread the cord through the casing and out through the same opening. Slide a cord lock on the cord ends and knot the two cords together. (Fig. 6) (If you prefer to make a double drawstring closure, follow the instructions on page 9.)

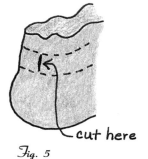

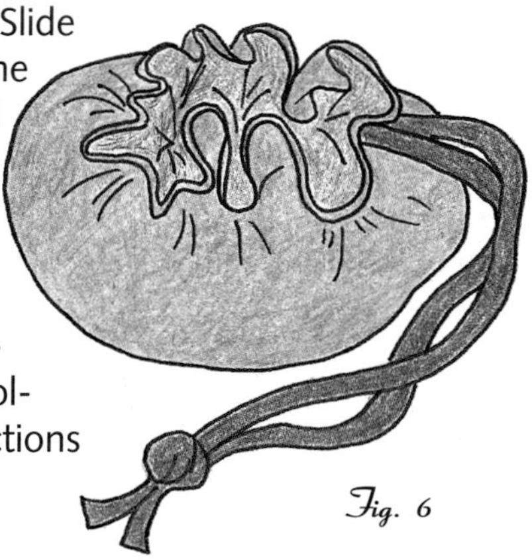

Fig. 6

Hint: After you trace and make the circle patterns for this project, store them in an envelope you glue or tape inside the cover of this book (a good place for all paper patterns you create for the projects in this book). Write a reminder note on the margin of this page so you can easily locate the pattern pieces and sew this bag in a jiffy.

Option: Line the jewelry bag with anti-tarnish fabric to protect silver and gold jewelry. The dark print bag on page 31 has this feature.

Cosmetic Bag

Store bathroom supplies for travel in this zippered cosmetic bag. Outside pockets hold last-minute additions such as tea bags for late night refreshments. Sandcastle quilted fabric by Dan River. Decorative trim and ribbon for handles from The RainShed.

CARRY YOUR BATHROOM SUPPLIES AND COSMETICS IN THIS EASY-TO-SEW BAG. THE LINING HAS EXTRA STORAGE POCKETS. USE MEDIUM WEIGHT FABRICS LIKE THE QUILTED FABRIC I CHOSE, OR TERRYCLOTH OR POLARFLEECE FOR A DURABLE, WASHABLE BAG.

Supplies:

½ yd. medium weight fabric for bag
6" x 14" piece of contrasting fabric for
    front pocket
½ yd. cotton or nylon fabric for lining
Zipper, 14" or longer
2 yd. decorative braid
2 yd. ribbon, slightly wider than the braid
4" piece of 1" elastic for bottle holder
    inside bag (optional)

Steps:

1. Cut fabrics and lining for the bag, as illustrated. (Fig. 1)

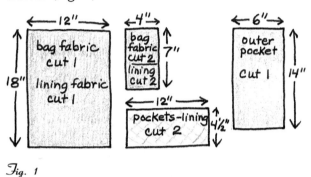

Fig. 1

2. Begin by sewing the lining for the bag. On the two pocket lining fabrics, zigzag across the top 12" edges, turn under ½", press, and sew across. Turn under ¼" on the bottom edge and press. (Fig. 2)

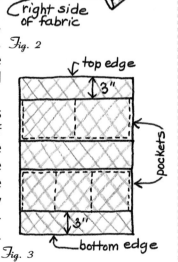

Fig. 2

Sew the pockets to the right side of the lining fabric, one 3" from the top edge and one 3" from the bottom edge. Sew divisions in the pockets to fit your needs. (Fig. 3)

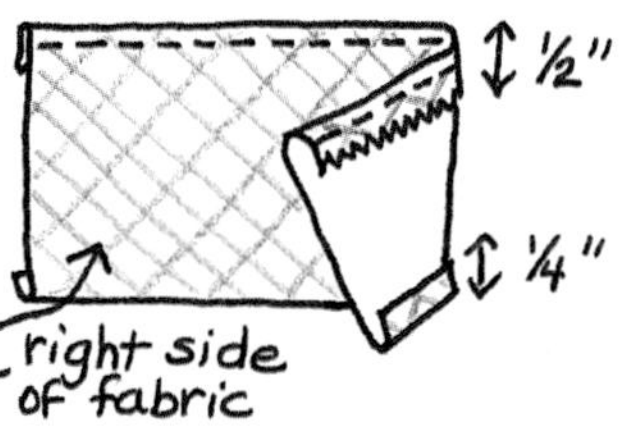

Fig. 3

3. To attach an elastic strip as a bottle holder, pin and sew the ends of the elastic to the right side of one of the lining side pieces 3" from the bottom edge. (Fig. 4)

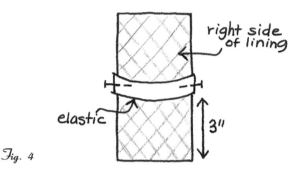

Fig. 4

4. Fit the side pieces to the lining by matching the bottom center of the sides to the center line of the main piece, with the right sides of the fabrics meeting. Sew the sides to the lining with a ¼" seam allowance. (Fig. 5)

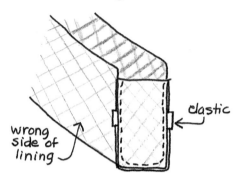

Fig. 5

At the corners of the side pieces, stop stitching and pivot the fabrics to turn the corners, or round the corners as you sew.

5. Assemble and sew the outer bag, starting with the pocket. Turn under the outer pocket fabric's 6" edges and sew across. Draw lines 3½" from each edge of the bag's outer fabric. Center the pocket piece on the right side of the bag along the lines and sew the pocket sides in place on the 14" edges. (Fig. 6)

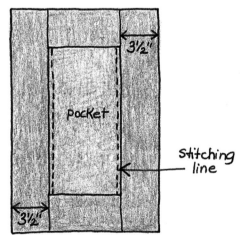

Fig. 6

6. To make the two-layer handle, sew the braid and ribbon pieces together. Begin pinning the handle strip to the bag at the bottom center line of the bag. Pin the strip edge along the pocket edges and up to 1½" from the top edges of the bag. Then measure 17" for the handle and pin the strip to the other side of the pocket 1½" from the edge. (Fig. 7)

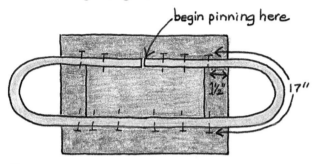

Fig. 7

Sew each handle strip to the bag, following your pins. (Fig. 8)

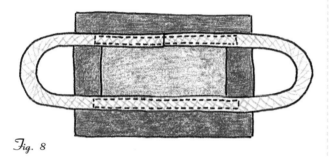

Fig. 8

7. Sew the bag sides to the bag fabric in the same way you sewed the lining pieces together (see Step 4).

8. Slide the lining over the outer bag with right sides together. Pin the top edges together and sew a ¼" seam, leaving an opening to turn the bag right side out. (Fig. 9)

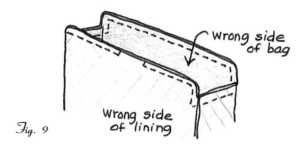

Fig. 9

Trim the seam allowance and also clip to the corners. (Fig 10)

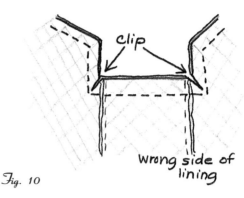

Fig. 10

Turn the bag right side out and tuck the lining inside the bag. Press the top edge of the bag.

9. On the top of the zipper, clip off the metal ends and turn under each end. (Fig. 11)

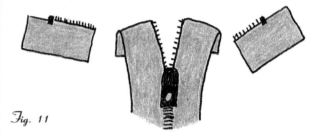

Fig. 11

Pin the edges of the zipper over the top long edges of the bag. Allow the end of the zipper to extend past the end of the fabric edges. Sew two seams on each side of the zipper to better secure the zipper to the long sides of the bag opening. (Fig. 12)

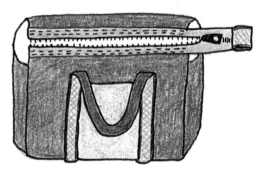

Fig. 12

10. Cut the zipper 2" longer than the fabric edge and wrap the end with an extra piece of ribbon trim or fabric as shown in Fig. 12. The extended zipper allows this bag to be opened wide for easy access.

Option: Personalize this bag with a monogram or machine embroidery on the outer pocket.

Placemat Bag

Sew Easy

Sew two placemats together to make this handy bag. The three zipper pockets hold lingerie, jewelry, scarves, cosmetics, medications, or a child's small toys. When you're ready to travel, fold up the bag and close it with an elastic loop, such as the ponytail loop featured on this bag, and an interesting button.

BUY TWO MATCHING PLACEMATS TO MAKE THIS BAG FOR STORING JEWELRY, LINGERIE, DOLL CLOTHES — YOU NAME IT. QUILTED OR THIN WOVEN PLACEMATS WORK BEST FOR THIS PROJECT.

Steps:

1. Pin the three zippers to the right side of one placemat at 1½", 6½", and 12½" lines. (Fig. 1)

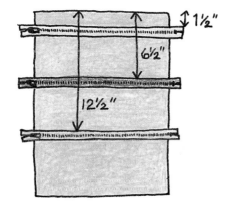

Fig. 1

Sew two seams around the length of each zipper for a secure hold. Cut off the zipper ends that extend beyond the placemat edges.

2. Sew the piece of ribbon ½" from the end of the zipper. Wrap the ribbon over the edge of the placemat and sew to secure. (Fig. 2) Cut off the ribbon and proceed to sew and wrap the other ends of the zippers in the same way.

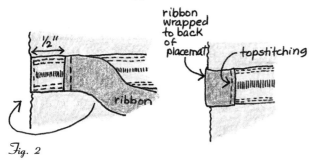

ribbon wrapped to back of placemat

topstitching

ribbon

Fig. 2

3. Cut the placemat fabric from behind the three zippers. (Fig. 3)

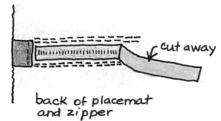

cut away

back of placemat and zipper

Fig. 3

4. Pin the two placemats together with wrong sides meeting. Insert the elastic hair loop between the top edges of the two placemats and sew across to secure. Make sure to avoid stitching on the metal section of the loop. (Fig. 4) Sew around the placemat edges.

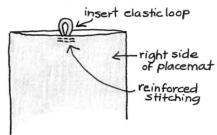

insert elastic loop

right side of placemat

reinforced stitching

Fig. 4

5. Sew divisions in the bag by stitching above the second and third zippers. Also sew vertical lines to create divided pockets in the bag. (Fig. 5)

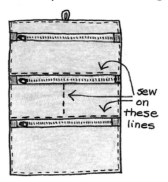

sew on these lines

Fig. 5

6. Fold the bag in thirds and plan the placement of the button with the loop closure.

Sew the button to the outer side of the bag. Add ties to the zipper heads to make the zippers easier to open and close (see page 9).

Options:

- Instead of using a placemat as the inside layer of the bag, use mesh fabric or vinyl so you can see into the pockets.
- Make this a roll-up bag by using two ribbon ties instead of the button and loop closure. Roll up the bag and tie it closed with the ribbons. (Fig. 6)

Fig. 6

Curling Iron Carrier

Cut apart and line a placemat with Teflon fabric for a classy and practical Curling Iron Carrier. Use the outer pockets to store the electric cord and a comb. Add a ribbon loop to hang the carrier from a bathroom hook or doorknob.

START WITH A PLACEMAT AND ADD TEFLON FABRIC AS A LINING TO MAKE A CURLING IRON CARRIER THAT'S STYLISH AND PRACTICAL TOO. WHILE IT'S STILL HOT FROM USE, STORE THE CURLING IRON IN THE CARRIER AND NO DAMAGE WILL BE DONE TO CLOTHING OR VINYL COSMETIC BAGS IN YOUR SUITCASE. THIS QUICK PROJECT MAKES A GREAT GIFT FOR ANYONE WHO USES A CURLING IRON. BUY QUILTED OR WOVEN PLACEMATS — OFTEN A BARGAIN IN THE TABLE LINENS DEPARTMENT — FOR THE FASTEST WAY TO SEW THIS CARRIER.

Supplies:

Placemat, 12"-13" x 18" or ½ yd.
  durable fabric
⅓ yd. or one piece 9" x 12" Teflon or
  Iron Quick fabric
2" piece of Velcro
10" ribbon for hanging loop

Steps:

1. Since placemats vary a bit in size, check the size of the curling iron on the placemat. Then cut 4¼" pieces off each side of the placemat. (Fig. 1)

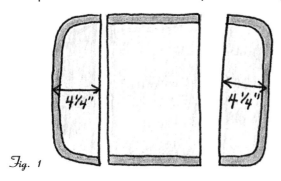

Fig. 1

2. Pin and sew the Teflon fabric to the wrong side of the center section of the placemat. (The shiny or silver side will be facing up and the wrong side of the Teflon will meet the wrong side of the placemat.) Sew Velcro halves to the top edge of the center section. (Fig. 2)

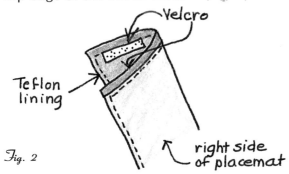

Fig. 2

3. With right sides up, pin the two side sections to the right side of the center section and sew on the sides and bottom edge of each piece, leaving the tops open for inserting the electric cord on one side and a comb or brush on the other. (Fig. 3)

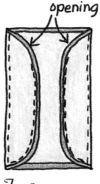

Fig. 3

4. Fold the center section with right sides together, pin, and sew only the raw edges on the sides together, reinforcing the stitching at the top and bottom of the seam. (Fig. 4)

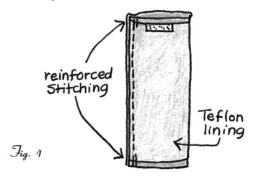

Fig. 4

5. Turn the carrier right side out. Sew across the bottom edges, stitching slowly through the thick layers. (Fig. 5)

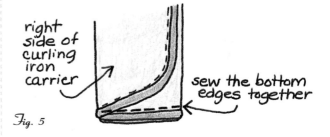

Fig. 5

6. Sew a piece of ribbon to the top edge of the carrier opening so this accessory can be hung on a bathroom or closet wall or doorknob.

Option: Add a monogram to personalize the carrier.

Travel Hint

On trips to foreign countries, bring a U.S. map and a map of your state. It will be easier to explain where you live and where other well-known cities are located. In addition, a few postcards of your city and photos of your family, car, and home, inside and out, will help you to describe your daily life to new friends and acquaintances.

Postcard Portfolio

Use the Postcard Portfolio and make it convenient to write and send postcards on your trip. Outside pockets hold stamps and address labels you write before leaving home. Store extra postcards in the inside pocket. Oilcloth fabric from Oilcloth International.

CARRY YOUR POSTCARDS AND STAMPS TO THE BEACH IN THIS QUICK-TO-MAKE OILCLOTH PORTFOLIO. THERE'S A POCKET ON THE BACK FOR STAMPS, A PEN, AND ADDRESS LABELS. CHOOSE OILCLOTH OR OTHER NON-FRAYING FABRICS SUCH AS ULTRASUEDE OR FELT.

Supplies:

½ yd. oilcloth (pieces of contrasting oil-
   cloth prints can be used) or other non-
   fraying fabric
Pinking shears (optional)
Cellophane tape
Teflon presser foot for sewing machine

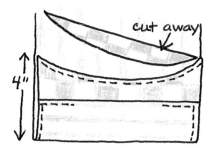

Steps:

1. Cut two pieces of oilcloth 7½" x 13". Cut one piece 7½" x 6" from the same or a complementary print fabric. (Fig. 1)

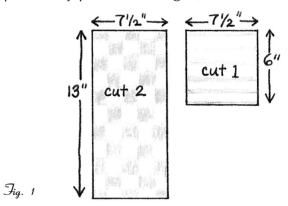

Fig. 1

2. On the 7½" x 6" piece, turn under ¼" and sew across each 7½" edge. Place this piece right side up 2" from one end of the right side of the outer piece of oilcloth. Use tape to hold the pieces together if you don't want to pin through the oilcloth. Sew the side edges to the larger piece of fabric and sew in 1½" from each edge at the top, as illustrated. The

Fig. 2

opening space between the stitching will be where the portfolio top flap is inserted. (Fig. 2)

3. Place the two main pieces of oilcloth with wrong sides together. Draw a slight curve across the end, as illustrated, and stitch through both layers of oilcloth on the line. (Fig. 3)

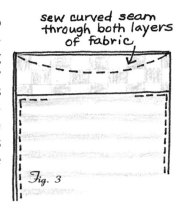

sew curved seam through both layers of fabric

Fig. 3

Trim close to the stitching line with scissors or pinking shears. Fold up 4" of the end with the pocket. (Fig. 4)

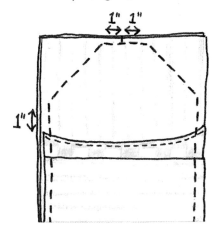

cut away

4"

Fig. 4

4. On the unfolded end that will form the portfolio flap, mark points 1" on each side of the center. Draw lines from the points to the sides of the portfolio, 1" above the pocket corner. Sew through the oilcloth layers ½" from the edge at the bottom edges and on the lines drawn on the flap. (Fig. 5)

1" 1"

1"

Fig. 5

5. Trim with scissors or pinking shears to even out the edges of all the pieces of oilcloth. Fill the portfolio with cards and supplies for writing messages at the beach or during your travels.

Hint: Instead of bringing an address book along, write or print out computer labels with the addresses of friends and family who would enjoy a travel postcard. This will save time and help you remember who still needs a greeting from your trip.

Option: Make the Postcard Portfolio from clear vinyl. The postcards and stamps stored inside will make the portfolio very colorful.

Traveling Desk

Choose a table runner as the base for a Traveling Desk. One tasseled end of the runner forms the top flap of the desk. The pockets sewn inside the desk hold a tablet and also the paper and office supplies you'll need while you're on the road.

SELECT A TABLE RUNNER WITH TAPERED ENDS FROM THE TABLE LINENS DEPARTMENT FOR THIS HANDY CARRIER OF PAPER AND DESK SUPPLIES. ONE RUNNER WILL HAVE ENOUGH FABRIC FOR TWO PROJECTS, WITH A LITTLE EXTRA FABRIC LEFT OVER IN THE MIDDLE. CONSIDER USING THE LEFT OVER FABRIC FOR A COORDINATING SMALL BAG SUCH AS THE BEDSIDE BAG ON PAGE 46.

Steps:

1. Cut the table runner to a length of 29". Turn the cut end of the runner under twice and sew across. (Fig. 1) If you are using a piece of fabric, fold in one end to form the taper.

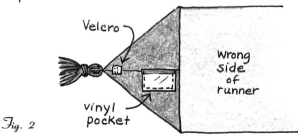

Fig. 1

2. To make it easy to sew a vinyl business card pocket on the table runner end flap, take out the stitches that hold the flap together on the center seamline and sew three sides of a 4½" x 2½" piece of vinyl on the back side of the runner's flap. To make the top edge of the vinyl more visible, sew a strip of bias tape binding to the vinyl before sewing it to the flap. Also sew a 1" piece of the rough or hook side of Velcro near the point of the flap. (Fig. 2) Re-sew the flap to the table runner on the center seamline.

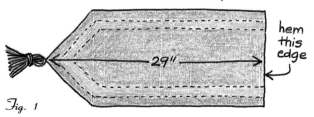

Fig. 2

3. Sew a 3" strip of the soft or loop side of Velcro 4½" from the outside edge and centered on the right side of the runner. (Fig. 3)

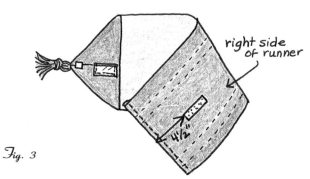

Fig. 3

4. Cut a piece of vinyl or mesh fabric 9½" x 12" for the tablet pocket. Place the pocket 8" from the end of the flap and sew around the sides and bottom, leaving the top open so you can slide the cardboard back of a legal tablet into the pocket. (Fig. 4)

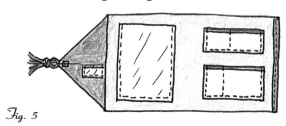

Fig. 4

5. Cut two storage pockets from vinyl or mesh fabric. They can be sized to fit the open space on the open side of the runner. I cut two pieces of mesh fabric 10" x 6", sewed bias tape binding to the top edges, and turned under the other three edges. (Fig. 5)

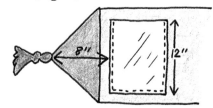

Fig. 5

6. Sew the pockets to the table runner and sew divisions in them to hold envelopes, note cards, and stamps. To hold small items securely inside the pockets, you may wish to sew narrow strips of Velcro to the binding and runner.

Options:

- Sew a loop of elastic or a narrow fabric pocket to the open space on the runner to hold a pen or pens.
- Pair this project with the Office Supply Kit on page 109 for two compact carriers of all the basics to set up and work on a hotel room desk.

Travel Hint

A fabric softener sheet inside a suitcase keeps it smelling fresh. Add a new sheet before a trip for an easy way to remove static cling by rubbing the sheet lightly on your clothing.

Bike Bag

Add easy-to-reach storage pockets to each side of the crossbar of your bicycle with this Bike Bag. Velcro wraps hold the bag in place. Cordura nylon fabric from The RainShed, zippers from A&E.

Supplies:

½ yd. sturdy fabric
Two zippers, 20" or longer
24" piece of Velcro
24" piece of ½" or ⅝" ribbon

Steps:

1. Trace and piece together the Bike Bag patterns from pages 121-122. Fit the paper pattern over the crossbar to check the size and shape. Adjust and change the shape at this time by adding to or cutting away from the paper pattern. Make sure to fit the pattern under the cables extending along the crossbar. (See photo) Mark the line where the top edge of the bag meets the body of the bag after wrapping it over the crossbar. (Fig. 1) This will be the guide for the placement of the Velcro.

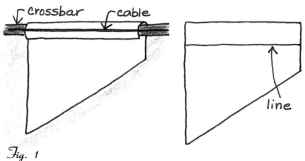

Fig. 1

2. Cut two pieces of fabric from the paper pattern, adding ¼" seam allowances on all edges. These pieces will be the base for the pockets

FOR BICYCLE TRIPS AROUND TOWN OR ON THE TRAILS, IT'S CONVENIENT TO STORE A FEW BASIC SUPPLIES IN A BAG THAT IS EASY TO REACH. THIS BAG FEATURES ZIPPERED POCKETS ON BOTH SIDES AND ATTACHES TO THE BICYCLE'S CROSSBAR WITH THE HELP OF VELCRO. MY RESEARCH OF BICYCLES SHOWS THAT EACH ONE HAS A DIFFERENT CROSSBAR DESIGN, SO THIS PROJECT MUST BE FIT TO A SPECIFIC BICYCLE. USE THE DIRECTIONS AND PATTERN PROVIDED AS A STARTING POINT TO SHAPE A BAG FOR YOUR OWN TWO-WHEEL VEHICLE. DURABLE FABRICS TO CONSIDER ARE CORDURA NYLON, CANVAS, OR OTHER STURDY WATER-REPELLENT FABRICS.

and for the top wrap around the crossbar. Mark the line for the Velcro placement on the right side of each piece of fabric. (Fig. 2)

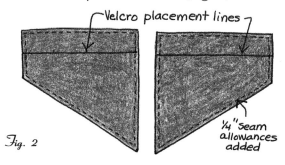

Velcro placement lines

¼" seam allowances added

Fig. 2

3. Use the line on the paper pattern as the top edge for the pocket pattern. Make a pocket pattern from paper by adding 1" above the line and 1" to the bottom edge of the pattern and keep the side edges equal to the bag pattern. Cut two pockets from fabric. (Fig. 3)

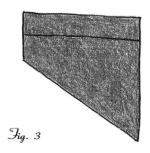

1"

pocket

1¼"

Fig. 3

4. Sew an exposed zipper to the right side of each pocket piece 1" below the top edges of the fabric. Follow the instructions on page 10 and cut out the fabric from behind the zipper teeth. (To reduce the zipper bulk at the ends of the zippers, use the ribbon or fabric end technique on page 47.) (Fig. 4)

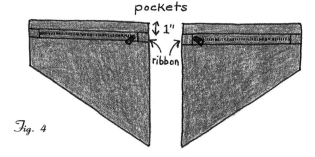

pockets

1"

ribbon

Fig. 4

5. Turn under the top pocket edge ¼" and pin on the line marked on the pocket base fabric. Pin the bottom edge of the pocket to the bottom edge

tuck

tucks

Fig. 5

of the base. On the sides, pin in tucks or pleats to match up the two edges. These tucks give extra depth to the pockets. Topstitch the pocket edges to the base fabric. (Fig. 5)

6. Cut pieces of ribbon or fabric to form straps to hold the bag edges to the lower and side bars of the bicycle. Wrap one side of the bag over the crossbar to determine where to sew the straps to the bag and use a tape measure to determine their length. Cut and pin the straps to the edges of one of the base fabrics. (Fig. 6)

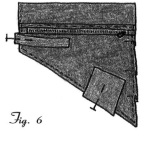

Fig. 6

7. Fit the two base fabrics together with right sides meeting. Sew ¼" seams around the sides and bottom, leaving the top edge open. (Fig. 7)
Clip and trim the seam allowances and turn the bag right side out. Turn under the top raw edges of the bag and sew across. (Fig. 8)

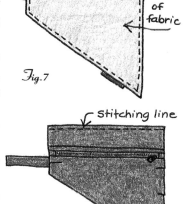

wrong side of fabric

Fig. 7

Stitching line

Fig. 8

8. Test the bag on the bicycle by wrapping and pinning it over the crossbar, and under, not over, the cables. Determine where the Velcro pieces should be sewn across the top edge of the bag and on the straps. Cut and sew the Velcro to the straps and bag.

9. Tie zipper pulls on the zipper heads (see page 9).

Hint: Attach the bag to your bicycle and fill it with a hat, sunscreen, a map, and a little money for a root beer float on your next biking trip.

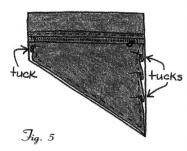

Option: Sew a 6" cord or fabric loop to the top corner of the bag so it's easy to hang and store when you remove it from the bike.

Bedside Bag

Collect bedside supplies in this simple-to-sew zippered bag. It's also a great cosmetics bag to carry inside a purse.

THIS SHAPELY BAG HOLDS A TRAVEL ALARM AND OTHER BEDSIDE SUPPLIES. IT'S SIMPLE TO SEW AND CAN BE MADE IN THREE DIFFERENT SIZES WITH THE PATTERNS IN THE BOOK. FOR THE BAG FEATURED HERE, THE SMALL SIZE PATTERN WAS USED. SEE THE MEDIUM SIZE PATTERN USED FOR THE FIRST-AID KIT ON PAGE 104. SUGGESTED FABRICS FOR THIS PROJECT ARE MEDIUM WEIGHTS: QUILTED FABRIC, TAPESTRY, CORDUROY, OILCLOTH, AND ULTRASUEDE. (THINNER FABRICS COULD BE MADE MORE SUBSTANTIAL WITH CRISP INTERFACING FUSED TO THE WRONG SIDE.)

Steps:

1. Trace the desired size Bedside Bag pattern from page 123 and cut two pieces of fabric to make the bag. Also cut a 1" x 3" strip of fabric or ribbon for the ends of the zipper. (Fig. 1)

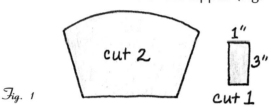

Fig. 1

cut 2

1"
3"
cut 1

2. Using this zipper method will eliminate bulk at the zipper ends and make it easier to sew the side seams. Cut the 3" fabric strip in half (1" x 1½") and sew one over the bottom end of the zipper, with the right side of the fabric facing the right side of the zipper. Make sure to avoid sewing on the metal bar. (Fig. 2)

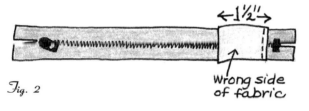

Fig. 2

←1½"→

Wrong side of fabric

Place the zipper along the curved edge of the bag fabric to plan where the second piece of fabric or ribbon will be sewn so

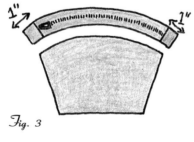

1"   1"

Fig. 3

that the zipper will have 1" tabs at each end when sewn to the bag top. (Fig. 3)

Pin and sew the fabric or ribbon strip to the top end of the zipper and trim away the excess zipper length on both ends. (Fig. 4)

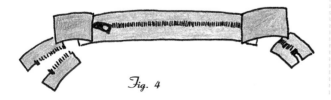

Fig. 4

3. Find the center point of the zipper and pin it to the center of the top edge of the bag with the right side of the zipper meeting the right side of the fabric. Sew the zipper to the fabric. (Fig. 5)

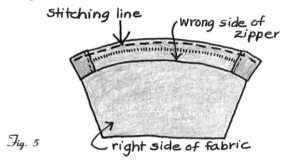

stitching line

Wrong side of zipper

Fig. 5

right side of fabric

Fold over the zipper so the unsewn side of the zipper meets the other side of the bag. Sew the zipper edge to the right side of the bag fabric. Topstitch through the zipper tape and the seam allowance from the right side of the bag. (Fig. 6)

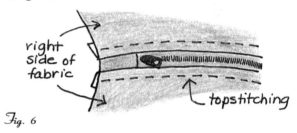

right side of fabric

Fig. 6

topstitching

4. Open the zipper a short distance. With the right sides of the bag together, pin the bag sides and bottom edge. Sew with a ¼" seam allowance. Fold in the bag corners to form a triangle and sew a 1" seam across each end, as explained on page 8. (Fig. 7)

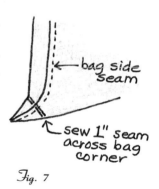

bag side seam

sew 1" seam across bag corner

Fig. 7

5. Turn the bag right side out. Add a zipper pull to the zipper head (see page 9).

Options:

• Sew pockets to the inside or outside of the bag.
• Add a monogram to personalize the bag.

Half-Circle Bags

Make Half-Circle Bags for men's and women's toiletries. Add a monogram for a personal touch. Sandcastle quilted fabrics by Dan River, nylon camouflage fabric from The RainShed.

HERE'S ANOTHER USEFUL BAG WITH AN INTERESTING SHAPE. USE IT AS A SMALL COSMETICS OR MAKEUP BAG OR TO STORE YOUR SHOE SHINE KIT (SEE PAGE 114). SUGGESTED FABRICS ARE MEDIUM WEIGHT. USE THE QUILTED FABRIC AND THE CAMOUFLAGE WATER REPELLENT NYLON SHOWN, OR CHOOSE TAPESTRY, TWILL, OR DENIM.

Supplies:

½ yd. medium weight fabric
Zipper, 16" or longer

Steps:

1. Trace the Half-Circle Bag pattern from page 124. Place the pattern on folded fabric or cut two pieces of fabric with a ¼" seam allowance added on the straight edge. Also cut two strips of fabric: 2½" x 16" and 2½" x 4". (Fig. 1)

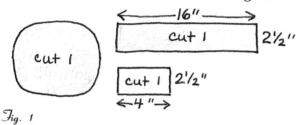

Fig. 1

2. Sew the zipper centered on the top right side of the 16" strip of fabric and cut away the fabric from behind the zipper teeth. Trim away the extra length of zipper on each end. (Fig. 2)

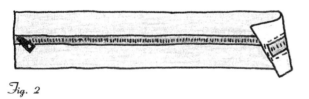

Fig. 2

Pin grabber tabs over the zipper ends (see page 9). Cut the 4" fabric strip in half and sew each piece over the ends of the zipper (and grabber tabs) to make a 17" long strip. (Fig. 3)

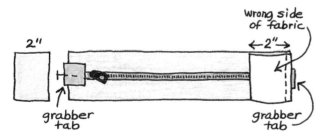

Fig. 3

3. Before assembling the bag, trim the bag front fabric with a monogram, machine embroidery, or a pocket.

4. Mark the center point along the length of the zipper piece on both sides of the fabric and also mark the center of the width of the short

ends. Open the zipper a short distance. Mark the quarter portions of the half-circle fabric piece. (Fig. 4)

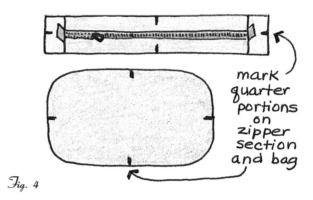

Fig. 4

With the right sides of the fabric together, pin the zipper fabric to the bag fabric, matching the bag fabric quarter portion marks to the zipper fabric center marks and pinning together all edges in between. Sew the 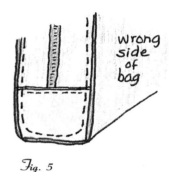 edges together with a ¼" seam allowance, rounding the corners at the bottom edge of the bag. (Fig. 5) Turn the bag right side out through the open zipper.

Fig. 5

5. Turn the seam allowances to the bag fabric and topstitch them in place from the right side of the bag. (Fig. 6)

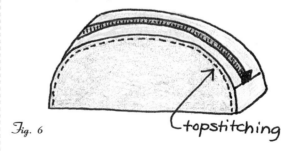

Fig. 6

6. Add a zipper pull to the zipper head (see page 9).

Option: Add piping to the bag fabric before sewing on the zipper fabric piece. See this detail on the camouflage bag and the Shoe Shine Kit bag on page 114.

Terrific Totes

Terrific Totes make great gifts! No woman ever has too many tote bags.

To all my friends

Tote in a Pocket

The front pocket of this handy tote bag has a dual purpose as a storage compartment for the bag. The tote is folded and stored inside the pocket, as seen on the right, and when it's opened, the full-size tote emerges. It's like magic! Pocket fabric by Marcus Brothers Textiles, purple nylon fabric from The RainShed, flowers from Mary's garden.

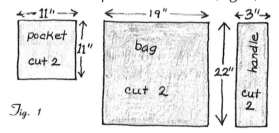

Supplies:

⅔ yd. 60"-wide nylon fabric
⅓ yd. cotton or other lightweight fabric for pocket
18" piece of ¾"-wide Velcro

Steps:

1. Cut two 11" squares of the pocket fabric. For the bag, cut two pieces of nylon fabric 19" x 22" and two pieces 3" x 22 ". (Fig. 1)

Fig. 1

2. Prepare the pocket first. Fold one square in half and press the fold line. On the right side of the fabric, draw lines ¾" from each edge. (Fig. 2)

Fig. 2

Cut one piece of Velcro 10" long and two pieces 4" long. Pin and sew the strips along the ¾" lines, with the soft or loop side of the Velcro on one

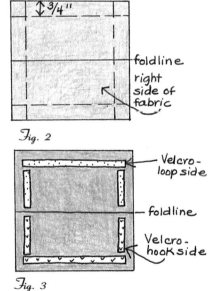

Fig. 3

THIS LIGHTWEIGHT NYLON TOTE BAG FOLDS UP TO BE STORED IN THE POCKET THAT DECORATES THE BAG FRONT. VELCRO STRIPS ON THE BACK EDGES OF THE POCKET HOLD THE FOLDED UP POCKET WITH THE TOTE BAG INSIDE. IT'S A CLEVER, COMPACT BAG THAT'S EASY TO STORE IN THE CAR OR YOUR SUITCASE AND IT'S A GREAT GIFT. FABRICS RECOMMENDED FOR THIS PROJECT ARE LIGHTWEIGHT NYLON, SUCH AS RIPSTOP OR SUPPLEX, AND, FOR THE POCKET ONLY, A COTTON PRINT FABRIC.

half of the square and the hook or rough strips on the opposite side. (Fig. 3)

3. Place the two pocket squares with right sides together and sew with a ¼" seam allowance. Leave an opening to turn the square right side out. (Fig. 4)

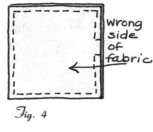

Fig. 4

Clip and trim the seam allowances, turn right side out, and sew the opening closed. The side with the Velcro strips will be the wrong or back

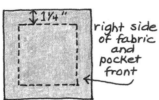

Fig. 5

side of the pocket square. Sew around the square 1¼" from the edges. (Fig. 5) Set the pocket aside while you sew the tote.

4. With the right sides of the tote fabric together, sew around the sides and bottom edges of the fabrics with a ¼" seam allowance. Sew the seam twice or with a reinforcing stitch on your sewing

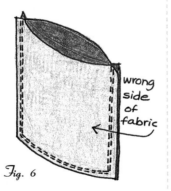

Fig. 6

machine to make a durable seam. If the nylon fabric ravels easily, zigzag the raw edges. (Fig. 6)

5. To form a rectangular bottom to the tote, follow the instructions on page 8. Measure a 6" line across the triangular folds at the bag corners and sew across on the lines. (Fig. 7) Reinforce these seams also.

Fig. 7

6. Sew the bag handles from the 3"-wide strips of fabric. Turn under ¼" on one long edge of each handle and press. Turn up the

Fig. 8

other edge 1" and overlap the ¼" edge over the raw edge. Press, pin, and sew. (Fig. 8)

7. Pin the handle ends 5" in from the side seams on each side of the bag. Sew across the ends ¼" from the edge. (Fig. 9)

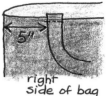

Fig. 9

Turn under the edge of the bag ½" and then 1". Pin and sew across the hem edges of the bag, reinforcing the stitching across the handles. (Fig. 10)

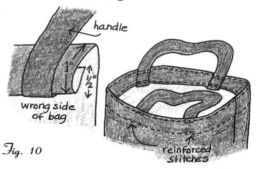

Fig. 10

8. Place and pin the pocket square (loop or soft side of Velcro closest to the bag's top edge) 2½" below the top edge of the bag and centered on the front. Sew along the

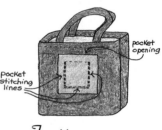

Fig. 11

sides and bottom stitching lines of the square, following the lines sewn earlier. (Fig. 11) Leave the top edge open so the square becomes a pocket.

9. Here's how to fold the tote into the pocket: With the pocket square down, fold the tote in thirds and then bring all edges inside the stitching lines on the pocket. Fold the pocket in half and match the Velcro sides together. (Fig. 12)

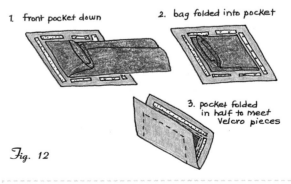

Fig. 12

Option: Think of all the decorating ideas you could apply to the pocket square: machine embroidery, monograms, applique, quilting, and more.

Rug-ged Tote

A lightweight rug makes a sturdy, washable tote bag. Add a front-entry zipper pocket for storing keys and other valuables. Note the button sewn to the side seam for a closure option for this tote bag. Decorative trim for the zipper pocket from The RainShed.

Supplies:

20" x 36" rug
48" webbing for bag handles
¼ yd. cotton fabric for pocket back and bag top edge facing
Zipper, 7" for front pocket
24" braid trim for zipper
Jeans needle or needle size 100 or 110
Button
6" length of cord, strip of Ultrasuede, or ponytail hair elastic for loop

Steps:

1. If the rug has fringed ends, cut off the fringe and immediately zigzag the edges. (Fig. 1)

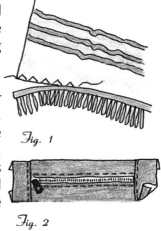

Fig. 1

2. To prepare the zipper opening for the tote, sew braid trim to the long sides of the zipper. Then sew braid across both the short ends and turn under the raw edge of the braid. (Fig. 2)

Fig. 2

3. Place, pin, and sew the framed zipper 3½" from the top edge of the rug. Sew two seams ¼" apart for a secure attachment. (Fig. 3) Cut away the rug from the back of the zipper area.

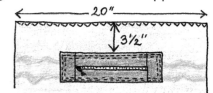

Fig. 3

CHOOSE A LIGHTWEIGHT WOVEN RUG FOR THIS PROJECT AND YOU'LL HAVE A VERY DURABLE TOTE BAG. MAKE SURE THE RUG ISN'T TOO THICK TO GET THE TWO LAYERS UNDER THE PRESSER FOOT OF YOUR SEWING MACHINE. THE EXTRA FEATURES OF THIS TOTE ARE THE FRONT OPENING ZIPPER POCKET AND AN OPTIONAL BUTTON AND LOOP CLOSURE FOR THE TOP OF THE BAG.

4. Cut two pieces of pocket fabric 11" x 10". Sew the fabrics with the right sides together and leave a small opening for turning. (Fig. 4)

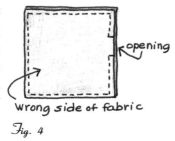

Fig. 4

Turn the fabric right side out and press. Position, pin, and sew the pocket backing on the wrong side of the rug behind the zipper opening. The top edge of the pocket backing should be slightly above the top edge of the framed zipper on the other side of the rug.

5. Fold the rug in half with wrong sides out and sew the two sides together to form the tote. (Fig. 5) To make box corners on the tote, follow the instructions on page 8.

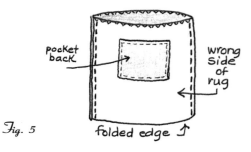

Fig. 5

Measure all around the top edge of the tote and cut a 2¼"-wide strip of fabric for the bag top facing, cutting it slightly longer than the bag measurement.

6. Pin and sew the right side of the facing to the right side of the tote. (Fig. 6)

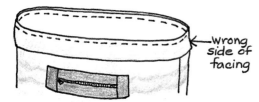

Fig. 6

Turn the facing to the wrong side of the tote and press. Turn under ¼" and press the other long edge of the facing. Pin the edge to the inside of the tote and sew around to secure the facing to the bag. (Fig. 7)

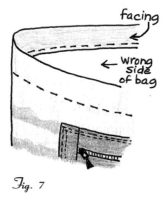

Fig. 7

7. Cut the handle webbing into two 24" pieces. Zigzag the cut ends. Position and sew the webbing ends 6" from each side seam. (Fig. 8)

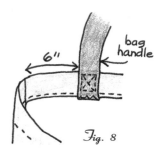

Fig. 8

8. Sew a loop of cord, Ultrasuede, or a ponytail elastic near the side seam inside the top edge of the bag. Sew a button on the outside of the tote on the opposite side seam. (Fig. 9)

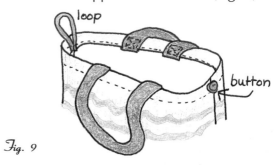

Fig. 9

Sew a fabric or cord loop to one side seam of the tote and a button to the opposite side seam for a quick way to gather together and close up the top of the tote.

*O*ptions:
- Sew extra pockets inside the tote for more storage options.
- Sew an extra loop inside the bag for a key chain holder.

Tote with Top Extension

You can overfill this tote bag, thanks to an extension that also zips closed. The pink tote on the left shows this feature; the extensions on the black and maroon bags are tucked inside. Outside pockets hold an umbrella or maps. Pink and black bag fabrics and handles from The RainShed.

ONE OF THE BEST FEATURES OF THIS TOTE BAG IS THAT IT GROWS TO HOLD MORE CARGO. THE OUTER POCKETS ARE HANDY ADDITIONS AND THE HANDLES MADE FROM COLORFUL BRAID ADD DECORATION. YOU'LL FIND THIS BAG A SMART CHOICE FOR AIR AND CAR TRAVEL AND FOR TRIPS TO THE BEACH. MAKE THIS BAG IN MEDIUM OR LARGE SIZE (THE LARGE BAG MEASUREMENTS ARE SHOWN IN PARENTHESES). RECOMMENDED FABRICS ARE STURDY, STRONG FABRICS SUCH AS DENIM, TWILL, CANVAS, CORDURA NYLON, UPHOLSTERY FABRIC, OR TAPESTRY.

Supplies:

1 yd. 60"-wide sturdy fabric or 1⅓ yd. 45"-wide sturdy fabric
Zipper, 16" (18" for large size) or longer
3 yd. (3¼ yd. for large size) webbing or decorative braid for bag handles
Sewing machine needle size 100 or 110

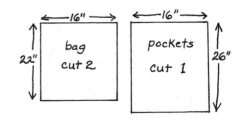

Fig. 1

16"
22" bag cut 2

16"
pockets cut 1 26"

If you prefer to sew fabric handles, cut two strips of fabric 3" x 52" (3" x 56") and follow the handle sewing instructions on page 8.

2. Make sure the sewing machine needle is the right size for the durable fabric you've chosen. Use a size 100 or 110 needle. Sew slowly and carefully, especially when sewing through multiple layers of fabric.

Steps:

1. Cut three pieces of fabric for the bag: two pieces 16" x 22" (18" x 24") and one pocket piece 16" x 26" (18" x 26"). (Fig. 1)

3. With the right sides of the two bag pieces together, sew across the bottom edges with a ¼" seam allowance. Sew a second seam to strengthen the stitching. (Fig. 2)

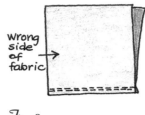

wrong side of fabric →

Fig. 2

4. On the pocket fabric, turn under and sew ¼" on the 16" (18") edges. Fold the fabric in half to find the center line that will be placed over the bottom seam of the bag.

5. Pin the pocket on the bag fabric with the wrong side of the pocket facing the right side of the bag and meeting the center line of the pocket and the seamline of the bag. Sew the

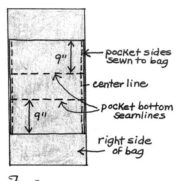

← pocket sides sewn to bag

← center line

← pocket bottom seamlines

← right side of bag

Fig. 3

pocket sides to the bag. Also sew across the pocket piece 9" from each open end. (Fig. 3)

6. Mark lines 5" from the bag side edges and 7" (8") from the bag top edge to guide the placement of the handles. Begin pinning the handle webbing at the bottom center of the bag, along the lines drawn on the bag sides. Pin the strip to the top edge mark, measure out 23" for the handle, and pin the webbing to the other side of the pocket. (Fig. 4) Overlap the ends of the handle webbing at the bottom of the bag.

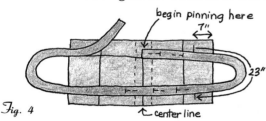

begin pinning here
7"
23"

Fig. 4

← center line

7. Sew the handles to the tote, stitching on both sides of the webbing and reinforcing the stitching across the handles. (Fig. 5)

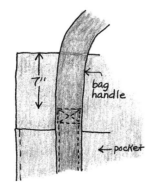

7"
bag handle
← pocket

Fig. 5

8. Turn under ¼" at the top edges of the bag, pin, and sew the zipper to the edges. (Fig. 6)

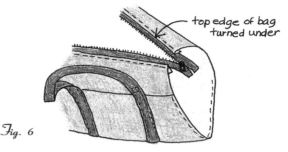

← top edge of bag turned under

Fig. 6

9. Sew the bag side seams with the right sides of the fabric together. Meet each side seam to the bottom seam and sew a 5" (6") seam across the triangular point formed when you meet the seams as explained on page 8. (Fig. 7)

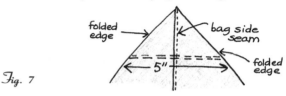

folded edge →
← bag side seam
← folded edge
5"

Fig. 7

10. To form the top edge of the open tote bag, mark a line 5" (6") below the zipper. Fold in and pin the top of the bag along the line and sew a ⅛" seam around the fold. (Fig. 8)

To extend the top of the tote bag, pull out the extra fabric tucked inside the bag. Zip the top closed to hold everything inside. (Fig. 9)

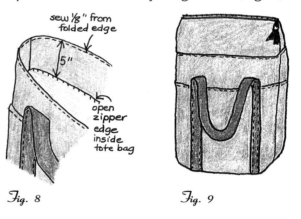

sew ⅛" from folded edge

5"

open zipper edge inside tote bag

Fig. 8   *Fig. 9*

*O*ption: Ellie's version of this tote includes a second handle on the top extension instead of a zipper. (Fig. 10) My thanks to Ellie and Dick for sharing this innovation!

Fig. 10

Backpack Purse

The front view of the Backpack Purse shows two zippered pockets and a short handle for carrying the bag like a purse. The main opening into the purse is on the back of the bag, presenting a secure and protected closure, especially when the bag is worn as a backpack. Tapestry fabric from The RainShed.

MAKE THIS SMALL AND COMPACT BAG TO WEAR ON YOUR BACK OR USE THE SHORT HANDLE AT THE TOP TO CARRY IT AS A PURSE. YOUR VALUABLES AND MONEY GO INTO THE BAG'S MAIN COMPARTMENT ON THE BACK SIDE, PROTECTED WHEN YOU WEAR THE BAG AS A BACKPACK. FABRICS FOR THIS PROJECT INCLUDE TAPESTRY, UPHOLSTERY, DENIM, ULTRASUEDE, AND OTHER DURABLE MATERIALS.

Supplies:

½ yd. sturdy fabric
18" square of lining fabric
4⅓ yd. ⅝"-wide grosgrain ribbon for
   backpack straps
14" length of ⅜"-wide grosgrain ribbon
   for bag handle
60" decorative trim for zipper edges
Four ½" D rings
Three zippers: one 9", and two 12"

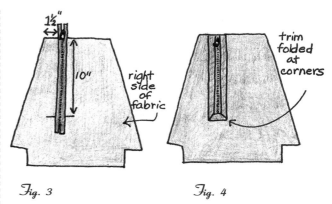

Fig. 3   *Fig. 4*

Steps:

1. Trace the two parts of the Backpack Purse pattern from page 125 and make a full size pattern on paper. Cut two bag pieces from the main fabric and one from lining fabric. (Fig. 1)

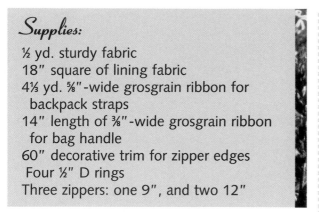

Fig. 1

2. On the right side of the pieces that will be the bag front, pin one zipper 1½" from the top edge and a second zipper 6½" from the top edge. (Fig. 2)

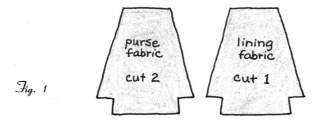

Fig. 2

Sew around both zippers, using the exposed zipper method on page 10. Sew trim along the sides of both zippers. Cut away the fabric from behind each zipper.

3. On the right side of the bag back piece, pin a zipper 1½" in from the left upper corner of the bag and straight down the fabric. Mark a line 10" down from the top edge of the fabric. (Fig. 3)

Sew the zipper onto the fabric and sew across the line drawn. Cut away the extra zipper length. Sew trim on the sides and across the bottom of the zipper, folding the trim at the corners. (Fig. 4)

4. Cut two strips of fabric 1½" x 8". These strips will reinforce the top edge of the bag. On the bag front piece, sew the strip to the wrong side of the top of the bag. This reinforcing piece will not be visible. On the bag back, sew the strip with the right side facing the right side of the bag and 1" from the top edge and over the end of the zipper. Pull the zipper head down below the stitching line across the fabric strip. Turn up and press the strip and sew it to the bag top edge. (Fig.5)

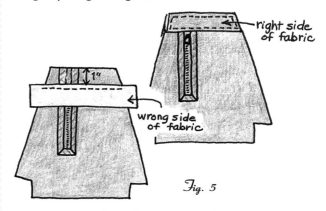

Fig. 5

Cut away the fabric behind the zipper on the back of the bag.

5. Place and pin the bag front and lining fabrics with the right side of the lining to the wrong side of the bag. Sew across the top edge of the lower zipper to form the upper pocket and across at the notched bottom edge to prevent

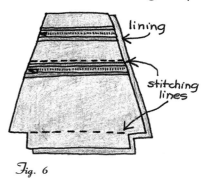

Fig. 6

items from getting lost on the bottom of the bag. (Fig. 6)

Sew the notched corners together on both the bag front and back fabrics, reinforcing the stitching. (Fig. 7)

Fig. 7

6. Make the bag handles and straps next. Fold the ⅜" ribbon in half lengthwise and sew both long edges. Pin the ends 1" from the bag edges on the top edge of the right side of the bag. (Fig. 8)

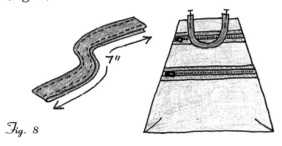

Fig. 8

Cut the 4⅓ yards of ⅜" ribbon in four pieces: two 66" long and two 12" long. Fold each ribbon in half lengthwise and sew along both long edges. (Fig. 9) You will have two 33" handles and two 6" ribbons for holding the D rings.

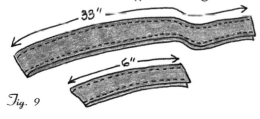

Fig. 9

7. Slide two D rings onto the two 6" ribbons. Pin the ribbons to the bag back ½" from the end of the bag corners. Place the raw edges of

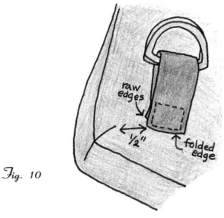

Fig. 10

the ribbons under the stitching area to attach the ribbons to the bag. (Fig. 10)

8. Pin the two long strap ends (raw edges) to the upper edge of the bag front. Sew across to secure. Pin the bag back and front together with right sides facing and matching the bag corners. Open the back zipper a short distance. Sew around the bag edges, sewing twice to reinforce the stitching. (Fig. 11)

Fig. 11

Trim the seam allowances and zigzag the edges if the fabric ravels easily. Pull the bag right side out through the zipper opening. Add ribbons or cord ties to each zipper head (see page 9). Adjust the length of the backpack straps with the D ring closures.

Option: Personalize this purse with a monogram using the alphabet on page 116.

Travel Hint

A large plastic garbage bag can serve many uses for a traveler: an emergency raincoat (with a hole cut in the closed end), a ground cover, a suitcase cover during a rainstorm, or a protective wrap for fragile items inside a suitcase.

Take-Along Accessories

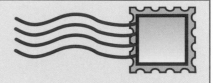

Take-Along Accessories carry important travel supplies. Choose distinctive colorful fabrics for a stylish impression.

To all my friends

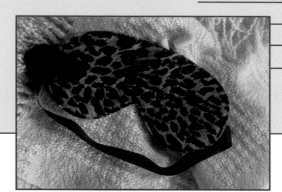

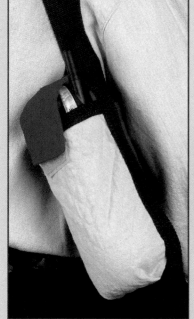

Traveling Tray

Here's one use for the Traveling Tray: a holder for cosmetics and toiletries in the bathroom. It also serves to temporarily store jewelry or money on a hotel room dresser. Open the tray corners, held in place by Velcro strips, and the tray becomes a flat piece that easily packs in a suitcase. Felt from Kunin Felt.

*S*EW A TRAY TO ORGANIZE COSMETICS, JEWELRY, OR MEDICATION WHILE YOU'RE ON THE ROAD. USE TWO PIECES OF NON-FRAY FELT FOR THE QUICKEST VERSION OF THE TRAY.

Steps:

1. Measure and mark a line 1¾" from each edge of the right side of one piece of felt. Place and pin the two pieces with wrong sides together. Sew around three sides, following the lines drawn on the felt and leaving one side open. (Fig. 1)

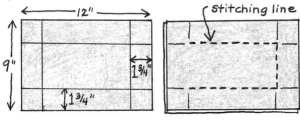

Fig. 1

2. Slide the piece of plastic canvas inside the opening between the two pieces of felt. Sew across the opening without catching the canvas in the stitching.

3. Cut the 2½" piece of Velcro into quarters, as illustrated. (Fig. 2)

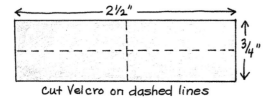

Fig. 2   Cut Velcro on dashed lines

Sew the matching hook and loop sides of the Velcro at each corner on the lines extending to the edges. (Fig. 3)

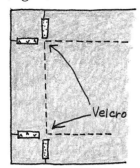

Fig. 3

4. Sew a ¼" seam around the top edges of the felt. Trim the edges with pinking shears.

5. Fold the corners up to match the Velcro strips and the flat pieces of felt become a tray.

Options:

- Use standard fabrics and cut the pieces 9½" x 12½". Sew a "pillowcase" and turn the fabrics right side out. Follow the directions in Steps 1 and 2 to complete the tray. After the plastic canvas is inserted and the opening is sewn closed, turn under the raw edges of the fabric end that is open and sew it closed.

- Make a tray for a trip to a potluck supper to hold your dish or dessert to share. For a 9" x 13" pan, I used two dish towels cut to 14½" x 20" and a piece of thin cotton quilt batting of the same size. After sewing the three layers together, with the batting in the center, I pinned the tray around the pan to test the placement of the Velcro strips. I used 3"-long strips of ¾" Velcro at each corner. This tray dresses up an ordinary pan and serves as a hot pad as well. Also consider using Teflon or Iron Quick fabric as the inside fabric for the tray.

Make a tray to hold a baking pan for your next trip to a potluck dinner. This tray is made from two dish towels and with its quilt batt lining, protects the table surface from a hot pan.

Travel Hint

Beware of hotel room bedspreads! They're usually made of dark, busy print fabrics and it's easy to lose valuable small items, like earrings and keys, on the bed. Make and use this Travel Tray and avoid placing any small items on the bedspread.

Potholder Eyeglass Case

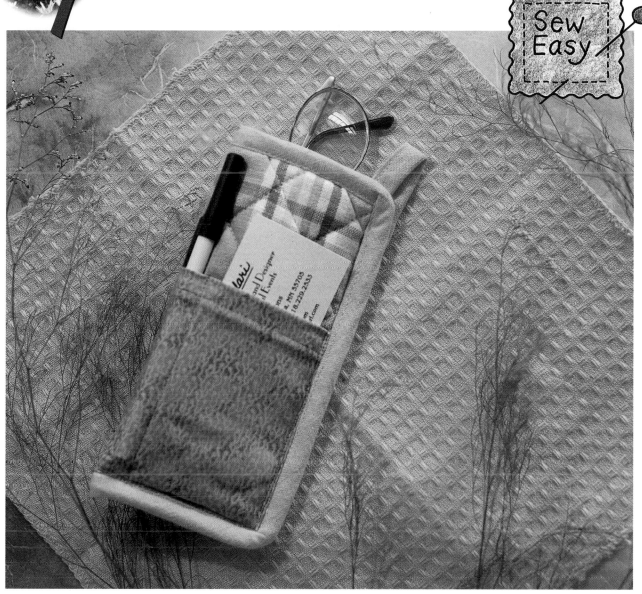

Sew fabric to a potholder to make a row of pockets on this eyeglass case. This quick-to-sew project starts off as a kitchen necessity and ends up as a practical and colorful accessory.

HERE'S A QUICK PROJECT AND A PRACTICAL GIFT: AN EYEGLASS HOLDER MADE FROM A POTHOLDER WITH AN ADDED ROW OF POCKETS FOR STORING ESSENTIALS. NEXT TIME YOU LOOK OVER KITCHEN LINENS AT THE DEPARTMENT STORE, LOOK FOR POTHOLDERS THAT WOULD MAKE INTERESTING EYEGLASS CASES. THE PADDING OF THE POTHOLDERS PROTECTS AND SUPPORTS THE EYEGLASSES STORED INSIDE.

Steps:

1. Prepare the potholder by removing the fabric loop at the top edge. Undo the stitching that holds the end of the loop in place and sew the fabric end to the wrong side of the potholder to remove the loop. (Fig. 1) (For the eyeglass case in the photo, I chose to keep the loop, which is sewn in the corner of the potholder.)

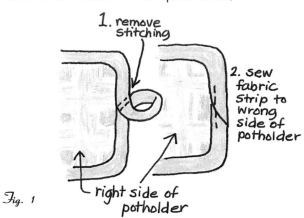

Fig. 1

2. Place the pocket fabric right side up over the right side of the potholder and trace the outline of the potholder to create the pocket shape on the fabric. Decide how deep you want the pocket to be and add a ¼" seam allowance to the sides and bottom edges and a 1" allowance to the top edge. (Fig. 2)

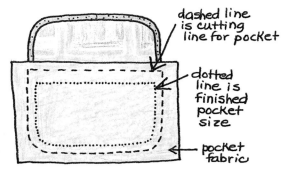

Fig. 2

3. On the top edge of the pocket, turn under the edge 1" and zigzag or serge the raw edge and sew across to secure it. Turn under and press the sides and bottom of the pocket piece. Pin to the bottom half of the potholder and sew in place. Sew divisions in the pocket for a key, a

pen, business cards, or other important items you want to carry. (Fig. 3)

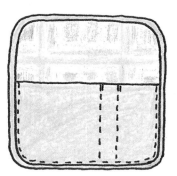

Fig. 3

4. Fold the potholder in half and use a size 100 needle to stitch the sides and bottom together, leaving 1" open near the top edge. (Fig. 4) This will be a thick seam, so sew slowly and make sure the sewing machine needle can handle the thickness.

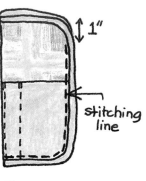

Fig. 4

Option: Leave the potholder loop in place and add a snap hook to attach the eyeglass holder to a tote bag or golf bag.

Travel Hint

Carry a copy of your eyeglass prescription when you travel, just in case you break or lose your glasses. Store it in one of the pockets of this eyeglass case and in a zipper pocket on the hanger cover (page 90).

*S*eatbelt Cushion

Sew a Polarfleece wrap for the seatbelts in your car and experience new comfort while driving and riding. The cushion slides on the seatbelt, removing the irritation of a seatbelt rubbing against the skin. Polarfleece by Malden Mills.

*S*upplies:

12" square of Polarfleece
11" piece of Velcro
12" piece of tear-away stabilizer

*S*teps:

1. Fold the piece of Polarfleece in half and pin the cut edges together on top of a piece of tear-away stabilizer. (Fig. 1)

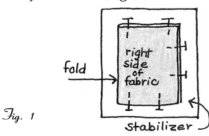

fold → right side of fabric

stabilizer

Fig. 1

2. Zigzag the three sides with cut edges together. (Fig. 2)

3. With stabilizer under the fabric, sew the soft or loop side of Velcro near the folded edge of the fabric. (Fig. 3)

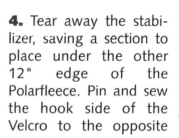

Stabilizer

Fig. 2

4. Tear away the stabilizer, saving a section to place under the other 12" edge of the Polarfleece. Pin and sew the hook side of the Velcro to the opposite

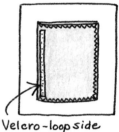

Velcro-loop side

Fig. 3

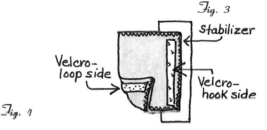

Velcro-loop side

Stabilizer

Velcro-hook side

Fig. 4

side of the fabric, as illustrated, with the stabilizer underneath. (Fig. 4)

Tear the stabilizer away and wrap the cushion around the seatbelt in your car. Make a second cushion for the car's passenger seat.

*O*ption: For infant seats in the car, cut the 12" cushion in half to wrap around the two straps that cross the baby's chest. It's more comfortable for tiny people too.

*W*RAP THIS ADJUSTABLE, SLIDING CUSHION OVER THE CAR SEATBELT AND ENJOY A MUCH MORE COMFORTABLE RIDE. THE SEATBELT WILL NO LONGER IRRITATE AS IT PRESSES ON YOUR BODY AND CLOTHING.

Map Holder

A perfect gift for the map reader on a car trip, this map holder is made from a placemat. Open the map holder to find a left side pocket for maps, pens, and maybe a magnifier. The vinyl-covered open pocket of the placemat holds the section of the map that needs to be in view.

Here's a perfect accessory for the map reader on any journey. This map holder is made with a placemat as the base. The clear vinyl window holds the portion of the map that is in use, while the zipper pocket on the side is perfect for additional maps, a pen, a magnifying glass, or a notepad.

Supplies:

Fabric placemat
¼ yd. coordinating fabric or matching
  dinner napkin
Zipper, 16"
3" piece of Velcro
12" x 14" piece of clear vinyl
12" ribbon or bias tape

Steps:

1. Fold the placemat in half horizontally with wrong sides together. Mark the center on the left edge of the placemat and mark the center 4" from the right edge. (Fig. 1)

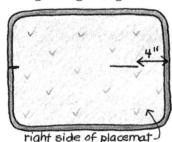

Fig. 1   right side of placemat

2. Sew the two sides of the Velcro to the placemat. On the left side, wrap the hook side of the Velcro with ½" over the edge to the wrong side. Pin and sew. On the right side, pin and sew the soft or loop side of Velcro 4" from the right edge, as illustrated. (Fig. 2)

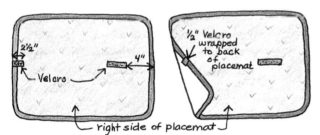

Fig. 2

3. Prepare the zipper pocket by cutting a piece of fabric 6½" wide and 1" longer than the actual height of the placemat. Pin and sew the zipper to the right side of the fabric 1" from the long edge. (Fig. 3)

   Cut away the fabric from behind the zipper teeth. Turn under the edge nearest the zipper ¼" and press. Turn

Fig. 3

under and pin the other three sides of the pocket fabric to fit inside the placemat edge. Sew around the pocket to attach it to the placemat. (Fig. 4)

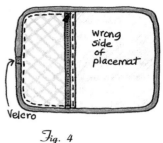

Fig. 4

4. Start with a piece of vinyl larger than the remaining open area of the placemat. Use a Teflon presser foot on the sewing machine so it will glide over rather than stick to the vinyl. Sew a strip of ribbon or bias tape binding on the right edge of the vinyl. Place the vinyl over the open space on the placemat, keeping the trimmed edge inside the placemat right edge. Pin the vinyl to the open space on the placemat, leaving excess vinyl on all edges except the right, bound edge and positioning the pins near the outer edges of the vinyl, as illustrated. (Fig. 5)

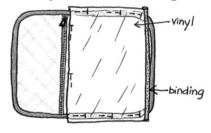

Fig. 5

   Sew around the three sides of the vinyl to form a pocket and trim away the excess vinyl beyond the stitching lines. (Fig. 6)

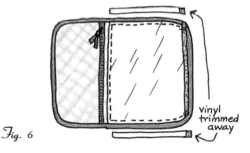

Fig. 6

5. Fold the map holder in thirds and secure with the Velcro. Your map holder is ready to use. Insert a map folded to show just the section you need to have visible. Fold back the zipper pocket and the Velcro on the back will hold it in place so the map section is the only part facing up.

Option: Make the zippered storage pocket from vinyl to see what's stored inside.

Blanket in a Pillow

Sew Easy

Above. A Polarfleece pillow stuffed with a blanket provides a comfortable way to relax in the car and a convenient place to store a blanket. Polarfleece by Malden Mills.

At left. Use the Polarfleece blanket on the sofa and stuff the pillow opening with another pillow. This accessory can also be used on a camping trip or in a college dormitory room. Polarfleece by Malden Mills.

KEEP THIS BLANKET STORED IN A PILLOW IN YOUR CAR, A SUMMER COTTAGE BEDROOM, OR A COLLEGE DORM ROOM. IT'S A QUICK-TO-SEW PROJECT WITH A VERY PRACTICAL USE.

Supplies:

60"-72" Polarfleece or Berber fabric
½ yd. Polarfleece for pillow
Pinking shears or wavy edge rotary cutter

Steps:

1. Trim the edges of the blanket fabric with pinking shears or a wavy edge rotary cutter, trimming away the selvage edges. You can also round the corners of the fabric. (Fig. 1)

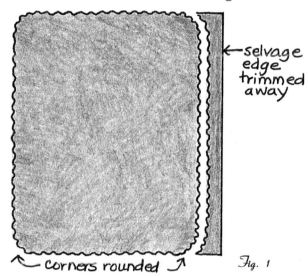

← selvage edge trimmed away

↖ Corners rounded ↗

Fig. 1

2. Cut one pillow piece 24" x 18". Mark lines 2" from each edge and sew on the lines. (Fig. 2)

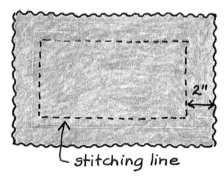

2"

└ stitching line

Fig. 2

Trim the edges of the pillow fabric with pinking shears or the wavy edge rotary cutter.

3. Place and pin the pillow fabric at the center of one 60" edge, lining up the top seamline with the top edge of the blanket. (Fig. 3)

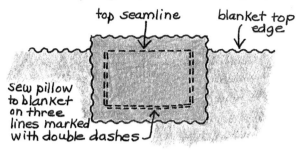

top seamline   blanket top edge

sew pillow to blanket on three lines marked with double dashes ┘

Fig. 3

Sew on the side and bottom lines you stitched, reinforcing the stitching at the top edge. The three stitching lines will form the pocket between the blanket and pillow fabrics.

4. To fit the blanket inside the pillow, place the pillow side down and fold the blanket in thirds, lining up the folds with the stitching lines on the side of the pillow. Next, turn the pillow side up, fold up the blanket from the bottom, and tuck it into the pocket between the pillow fabric and the blanket. (Fig. 4)

1. pillow side down

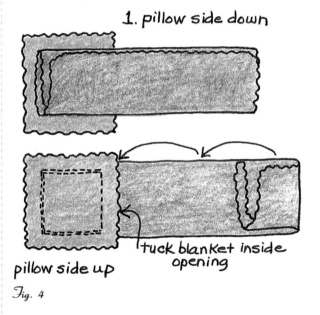

pillow side up

tuck blanket inside opening

Fig. 4

Option: Make a blanket sized for a child with a 54" x 60" piece of Polarfleece for the blanket and a 15" x 17" pillow.

Eyeshade

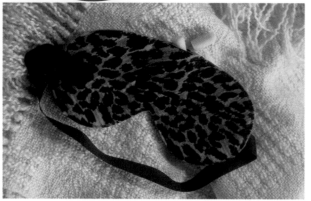

For a classy, unique eyeshade, choose animal print felt. A pocket opening at the top center edge holds a pair of foam earplugs for a quiet, restful nap. Felt by Kunin Felt.

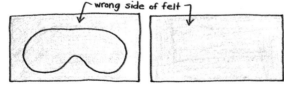

Supplies:

9" x 12" piece of felt
20" piece of ⅝" ribbon
3" piece of Velcro
Foam ear plugs (optional)

Steps:

1. Trace the Eyeshade pattern from page 126. Trace the shape near the top edge of the wrong side of the felt. Cut the felt in two pieces ½" below the bottom edge of the eyeshade tracing. (Fig. 1)

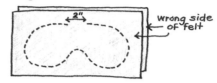

wrong side of felt

Fig. 1

2. Pin the two layers of felt together with the right side of the traced layer facing the wrong side of the other layer. Sew on the traced line, leaving a 2" opening at the top center of the eyeshade. (Fig. 2)

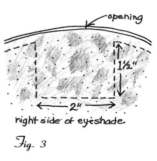

2"

wrong side of felt

Fig. 2

Trim away the extra felt, cutting ⅛" from the stitching line.

3. To form the storage pocket for the earplugs, mark and sew lines 1½" down from the ends of the open seam and another line 2" across, stitching through both layers of felt. (Fig. 3)

opening

1½"

2"

right side of eyeshade.

Fig. 3

Cut a narrow piece of Velcro to sew on both sides of the top opening of the eyeshade.

4. Sew one end of the ribbon to the center of one side of the eyeshade. Try the eyeshade on to determine the length of ribbon needed to go around your head and cut the ribbon 2" longer than the measurement. Fold back the open end of the ribbon 1½" and sew one side of a 2" piece of Velcro to it. Sew a square of Velcro to the right side and center of the eyeshade edge. (Fig. 4)

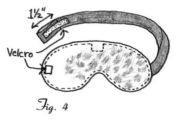

1½"

Velcro

Fig. 4

MAKE A CLASSY EYESHADE FOR A TRANSCONTINENTAL FLIGHT OR A STAY IN THE SCANDINAVIAN COUNTRIES OR ALASKA DURING THE SUMMER MONTHS OF THE "MIDNIGHT SUN." I CHOSE ANIMAL PRINT FELT FOR A FUN FABRIC. THERE'S A HIDDEN STORAGE POCKET FOR FOAM EARPLUGS AT THE TOP CENTER OF THE EYESHADE. REST IN COMFORT AS YOU WEAR THIS EYESHADE AND THE EARPLUGS TO BLOCK OUT SIGHTS AND SOUNDS ON A LONG NOISY JOURNEY.

Traveler's Photo Frame

Travel with pictures of the special people at home. This double picture frame is covered with vinyl and another piece of vinyl forms a pocket on the outside of the frame, ready to hold special notes for the traveler. The people in the pictures? My sister Becky, her husband Jes, and son Matti. Oilcloth by Oilcloth International.

Supplies:

¼ yd. non-fraying fabric
¼ yd. clear vinyl
12" length of narrow ribbon or bias tape
Cellophane tape

Steps:

1. Cut a piece of oilcloth and a piece of vinyl, each 8" x 12". Cut one additional vinyl piece 4" x 12" if you plan to have a pocket on the front of the frames for notes. (Fig. 1)

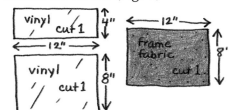

Fig. 1

2. If you're including the pocket, sew ribbon or bias tape to one 12" edge of the 4"-wide piece of vinyl. Then sew the sides and bottom edges of this vinyl piece to the right side of the frame fabric. (Fig. 2)

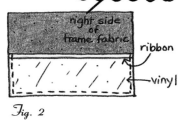

Fig. 2

3. Place the larger vinyl piece on the wrong side of the frame fabric. Hold the two layers in place with tape if you don't want to pin through the fabrics. Mark a ½" space at the center of the vinyl by drawing lines with a pen. (Fig. 3)

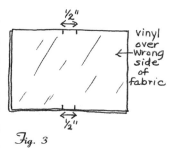

Fig. 3

4. Sew around the three outer edges of each frame space with a ¼" seam allowance. Start and stop the stitching at the ½" space and reinforce the stitching there. Carefully cut away the ½" strip of vinyl at the center. (Fig. 4)

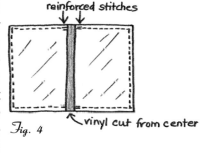

Fig. 4

5. Insert 3" x 5" photos that are in precut photo mats or insert a piece of thin cardboard behind 5" x 7" photos.

CARRY FAVORITE FAMILY PHOTOS TO DISPLAY ON THE BEDSIDE TABLE WHEN YOU'RE AWAY FROM HOME. THIS EASY-SEW SET OF FRAMES IS SIZED FOR 5" X 7" PHOTOS OR 3" X 5" PHOTOS IN MATS. THE OUTER VINYL POCKET HOLDS SPECIAL NOTES FROM THE FAMILY. THE EASIEST FABRICS FOR THIS PROJECT ARE NON-FRAY CHOICES SUCH AS OILCLOTH, FELT, OR ULTRASUEDE.

Ice-Cream Bucket Tote

Turn a plastic ice-cream bucket into a bath and shower supply carrier. Mesh pockets that hang on the outside of the bucket will hold more bottles and toiletries than what will fit inside the bucket. Nylon and mesh fabrics from The RainShed.

Supplies:

½ yd. nylon fabric
¼ yd. mesh fabric
1 yd. bias tape binding
Empty 5-quart ice-cream bucket or other plastic pail

Steps:

1. Trace the bottom of the ice-cream bucket or other pail and add ¼" all around, or use the Ice-Cream Bucket pattern on page 127. Measure around the top and bottom edges of the bucket and add ½" to each measurement. (Most buckets taper down from the top edge.) Also measure the depth of the bucket and add 1". Draw a tapered rectangle using these measurements.

2. Cut one nylon fabric circle for the bottom of the bucket lining and one nylon rectangle for the lining sides. (Fig. 1)

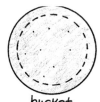

bucket bottom (dashed line) with ¼" added

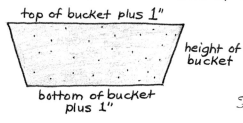

top of bucket plus 1"

height of bucket

bottom of bucket plus 1"

Fig. 1

CARRY THIS BUCKET, WITH ITS LINING AND EXTRA POCKETS, WHEN YOU VISIT THE SHOWER ROOM AT THE CAMPGROUND OR THE COLLEGE DORM BATHROOM. MAKE ONE FOR THE GUEST BEDROOM OR A RECREATIONAL VEHICLE. BESIDES ICE-CREAM BUCKETS, CONSIDER PLASTIC CONTAINERS FROM PRODUCTS LIKE COOKIES OR PRETZELS, OR BUCKETS FROM THE DOLLAR STORE. BUCKETS WITH OR WITHOUT HANDLES CAN BE USED FOR THIS PROJECT. SELECT NYLON FABRIC, WITH MESH FABRIC FOR THE OUTSIDE POCKETS.

Sew the tapered ends of the fabric strip with right sides together and a ¼" seam allowance. Mark quarter portions on both the circle of fabric and the fabric piece that is now a tube.

3. Pin and sew the tube to the circle, matching the marks and with the right sides of the fabric together. (Fig. 2) Fit this nylon insert inside the bucket to check the size and fit.

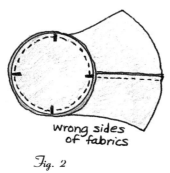

wrong sides of fabrics

Fig. 2

4. To make the pockets on the outside of the bucket, cut two pieces of nylon fabric 6" wide by half the top edge measurement plus 1". Cut two pieces of mesh fabric or other pocket fabric 4½" wide by half the top measurement plus 4". (Fig. 3)

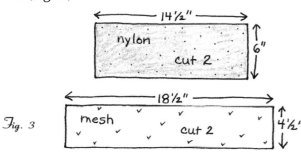

Fig. 3

Sew a piece of bias binding across one long edge of each piece of mesh.

5. Turn under the side edges of each pocket fabric twice and sew. Place the mesh fabric on the wrong side of the pocket section, pinning the sides of the mesh and fabric together. (Fig. 4)

mesh fabric

wrong side of nylon

Fig. 4

Pin four pleats or tucks in the bottom edge of the mesh, one pleat for each pocket division to be sewn in the mesh fabric. (Fig. 5)

wrong side of fabric

Fig. 5

Sew the sides and bottom edges of the mesh and pocket fabrics together and turn the pockets right side out. Sew up the pocket division lines to create individual pockets. (Fig. 6)

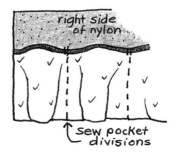

right side of nylon

Sew pocket divisions

Fig. 6

6. Meet the right side of the top edges of the two pocket sections to the right side of the top edge of the bucket insert fabric. (Fig. 7)

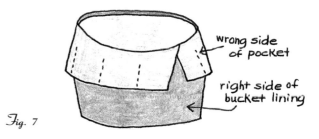

wrong side of pocket

right side of bucket lining

Fig. 7

Overlap the two pocket ends and pin the top edges together all the way around. Sew with a ¼" seam allowance and reinforce the stitching by sewing around twice or selecting a reinforced repeating stitch on your sewing machine.

7. Fit the liner inside the bucket with the handles between the two outer pocket sections. (Fig. 8) Load it with shower and bathroom supplies.

Fig. 8

Option: Make this bucket tote for craft or painting supplies.

Cell Phone Case

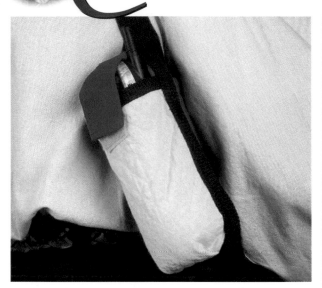

Slide this cell phone holder on the strap of your briefcase or bag for easy access when the phone rings. Sandcastle quilted fabrics by Dan River.

Supplies:

¼ yd. sturdy fabric or small pieces of various fabrics for the patchwork effect seen in the photo

1¼ yd. binding or double width bias binding

6" piece of Velcro

Front   Back

Steps:

1. Cut two 3½" x 7" pieces of fabric for the base, one 6" x 5" piece for the pocket, one 5½" x 9½" piece for the back wrap, and one 2" x 3" piece for the tab. (Fig. 1)

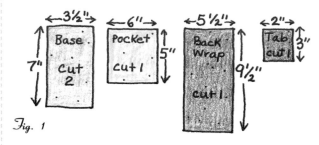

Fig. 1

2. Fold the back wrap fabric in half with wrong sides facing, so it measures 4¾" x 5½". Round out the corners for ease in wrapping the binding. This is especially important for the wider binding shown in the photo. Sew the binding to the fabric edges so the two layers are attached. (Fig. 2)

Fig. 2

3. Sew the wrap piece to the right side of the back layer of the base fabric, placing the top of the wrap 1" below the top edge and sewing 1" from each side, as illustrated. (Fig. 3)

Sew Velcro to the overlapping sides of the wrap and close the wrap to keep the edges out of the way while assembling the case. (Fig. 4)

Attach your phone to your briefcase or tote bag handle to keep it handy and easy to reach. This phone holder easily holds Nokia phones that are 5½" in diameter and 5½" tall with a 1" antenna extending. Larger size phones would fit also. Choose sturdy fabrics for this case. Denim, nylon, upholstery fabric, and quilted fabrics are suggestions.

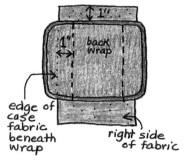

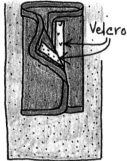

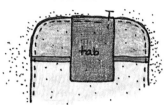

Fig. 3

Fig. 4

seamline is flat and centered. Sew across the tab end. (Fig. 8) Turn the tab right side out and press.

7. Pin the raw edges of the tab to the top edge of the base and sew close to the edge. (Fig. 9)

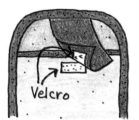

Fig. 9

4. Match the two layers of the base fabric with the wrong sides of the fabric together. Round off the four corners. Sew around the edges to hold both layers together. (Fig. 5)

Fig. 5

8. Wrap, pin, and sew the binding to the edges of the base. Meet the ends of the binding at the bottom center of the case. If it is difficult to have a neat overlap of the binding, cut a 1¼" square of Ultrasuede and wrap and sew it around the ends of the binding. (Fig. 10)

5. Sew binding across one 5" edge of the pocket fabric. Then sew a 1½" strip of Velcro ¾" below the edge of the fabric and centered. (Fig. 6)

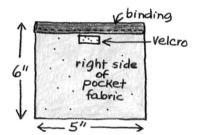

Fig. 6

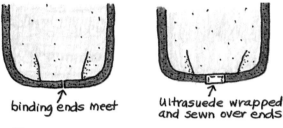

binding ends meet

Ultrasuede wrapped and sewn over ends

Fig. 10

9. Insert the phone in the case to determine the fit and the placement of the Velcro on the end of the tab. Sew a 1½" piece of Velcro on the tab. (Fig. 11)

Pin the two 6" edges to the edges of the front of the base. Fold in pleats to fit and pin the bottom edge to the base. Trim away the two bottom corners to match the base corners. (Fig. 7)

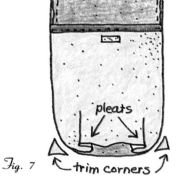

Fig. 7

pleats

trim corners

Sew around the pocket close to the edges of the fabric to secure the pocket to the base.

6. Fold the top tab fabric piece in half, with the right sides of the fabric together, to meet the 3" edges. Sew a ¼" seam. Refold the tab so the

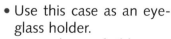

Velcro

Fig. 11

Options:

- For a stiffer base, use a piece of crisp interfacing between the two layers of base fabric.
- Use this case as an eyeglass holder.
- Sew a loop of ribbon or cord to the top edge of the case for another carrying option. (Fig. 12)

Fig. 12

Fig. 8

Luggage Tags

Large, colorful luggage tags help you identify your suitcases on the airport baggage carousel. The vinyl pocket on the front holds a business card or name tag. Make sure to sew the ties securely to the tags so they won't tear away. Oilcloth by Oilcloth International, yellow fabric from Marcus Brothers Textiles.

IT'S EASY TO IDENTIFY YOUR LUGGAGE WITH THESE EXTRA-LARGE TAGS. THEY'RE FAST TO SEW, AND WITH BRIGHT COLORFUL FABRICS, BECOME AN ATTRACTIVE ACCENT ON SUITCASES AND DUFFEL BAGS. FABRICS TO CONSIDER INCLUDE OILCLOTH, FELT, COTTON, AND ULTRASUEDE.

Supplies:

- 8" x 6½" piece of fabric
- 2½" x 4½" piece of clear vinyl
- 4" x 6" piece of interfacing or thin quilt batting for lining
- 18" non-slip cord, shoelace, or fabric strip for ties

Steps:

1. Trace the Luggage Tag pattern from page 126. Note that the outer edge of the pattern is the stitching line.

2. Trace the pattern shape on the wrong side of the fabric. Fold the fabric in half with the right sides meeting. (Fig. 1)

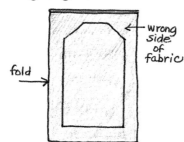

Fig. 1

3. Cut the piece of cord in half and insert and pin the two pieces at the top center point of the tag between the pieces of fabric. Place the lining piece under the fabrics. (Fig. 2)

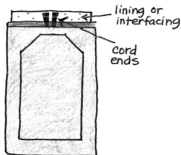

Fig. 2

4. Sew around the pattern line, reinforcing the stitching across the tie ends. Leave an opening at the short end, as illustrated. (Fig. 3)

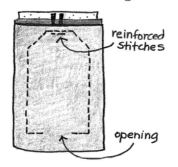

Fig. 3

Trim the seam allowances and turn the fabrics right side out. Press the edges and sew around all sides, about ⅛" from the edge, again reinforcing the stitching over the ends of the ties. (Fig. 4)

Fig. 4

5. Center and sew the vinyl on one side of the tag, sewing on three sides of the vinyl. (Fig. 5)

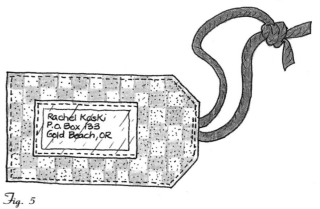

Fig. 5

6. Insert a business card or write your name and address on a 2" x 3½" piece of paper and insert it into the vinyl pocket.

Option: When using non-fray fabrics such as oilcloth or felt, trace the pattern on the right side of one piece of fabric. Place the wrong sides of the fabrics together, with the lining and cord ties in between. Sew on the pattern line traced on the fabric. Trim the edges with scissors or pinking shears.

Travel Hint

If you like to buy posters or unframed prints when you travel, pack the cardboard tube from a roll of gift wrap. You'll be able to roll and store posters both inside and outside the tube. Also bring along three or four rubber bands to hold the posters on the tube.

Bag Handle Wraps

Sew Easy

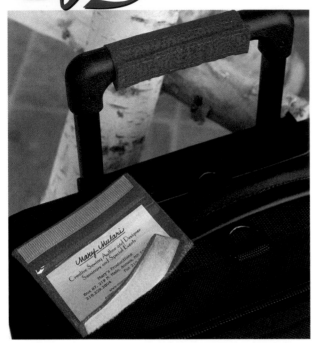

Brightly colored bag handle wraps clearly identify your luggage. Velcro holds the wraps in place and inside the wrap is a vinyl pocket for holding identification or a business card. Fabrics by Marcus Brothers Textiles.

Supplies:

Two 5" x 6" pieces of fabric
4" piece of Velcro
2½" x 4" piece of clear vinyl

Steps:

1. Pin the two 5" x 6" pieces of fabric with right sides together and sew around the edges with a ¼" seam allowance. Leave an opening to turn the fabric right side out. (Fig. 1)

Fig. 1

2. Trim and clip the seams and corners. Turn the fabric right side out and press. Sew the two pieces of Velcro on opposite 5" edges of the fabric. (Fig. 2)

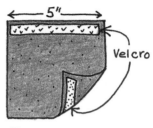

Fig. 2

3. Center the vinyl piece on the wrong side of the tag (the side with the loop strip of Velcro) and sew around three sides. Insert a business card or a piece of paper with the bag owner's name and address and/or phone number. (Fig. 3)

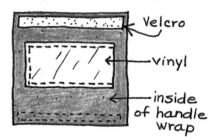

Fig. 3

Easy, isn't it? Make one of these for everyone on your gift list who owns a suitcase.

Option: For extra padding inside the handle wrap, add a layer of thin quilt batting or make the handle wrap from a piece of sheepskin. With extra layers of thickness, you may need to cut the fabric pieces longer than 6".

HERE'S ANOTHER WAY TO QUICKLY IDENTIFY YOUR LUGGAGE AS IT CIRCLES ON THE LUGGAGE CAROUSEL AT THE AIRPORT. ADD THESE FABRIC WRAPS TO THE HANDLES. COLORFUL COTTON FABRICS ARE A GOOD CHOICE FOR THIS PROJECT.

Safe and Secure Bags

Safe and Secure Bags hide and protect money and other valuables on your journeys.

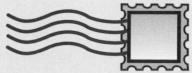

To all my friends

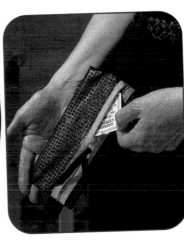

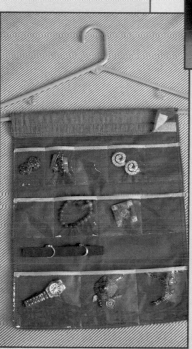

Pin-In Pocket

Sew a movable inside pocket for a jacket or another piece of clothing. Safety pins hold the pocket in place and the pocket holds a hotel room key, money, lipstick, or other important supplies. Pin the pocket to the garment side opposite your dominant hand for the easiest access. Cotton fabric from Marcus Brothers Textiles.

MOVE THIS POCKET FROM ONE GARMENT TO ANOTHER. USE SAFETY PINS TO SECURE IT TO A WAISTBAND OR INSIDE A JACKET. MAKE THE POCKET TO FIT YOUR NEEDS. THE POCKET SIZE FEATURED HERE HOLDS A PASSPORT AND OTHER ITEMS. FABRICS SUGGESTED FOR THIS PROJECT ARE COTTON, LIGHTWEIGHT NYLON, TENCEL, AND SILK.

Supplies:

⅓ yd. lightweight fabric
1" piece of Velcro
Two medium size safety pins

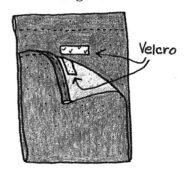

Steps:

1. Cut two pieces of fabric: one 6" x 8" and one 6" x 10". (Fig. 1)

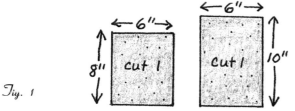

Fig. 1

2. On the 8" long piece, turn under twice, press, and sew a narrow hem across the top 6" edge. On the 10" piece, fold back a 1" hem to the wrong side of the fabric and sew it in place. (Fig. 2) This hem will support the safety pins that hold the pocket to the garment.

Fig. 2

right side of fabric

3. Sew the two fabrics together by pinning the two 6" unfinished edges together with the wrong sides facing up, as illustrated. (Fig. 3)

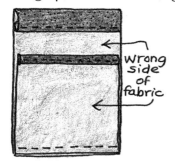

Fig. 3

Wrong side of fabric

Press the seam and fold the smaller fabric over the right side of the second fabric.

4. Sew a piece of Velcro to the inside top edge of the pocket and the matching piece of Velcro on the back fabric. (Fig. 4)

Velcro

Fig. 4

5. Pin the two fabrics together on each side. Zigzag the raw edges, then turn the edges to the back of the pocket and sew them in place. (Fig. 5) Add two safety pins to the hem at the top of the pocket and you're all finished.

wrong side of pocket

Fig. 5

zigzag and hem the sides

Option: When you're not using the pin-in pockets you've made for yourself, share them with traveling friends. You'll enjoy owning and sharing accessories that have traveled all over the world.

Travel Hint

To refresh stale air in a hotel room, carry a small candle in a metal container with a lid. Always make sure to blow out the candle when you leave the room and be responsible about tending it while it's burning.

Ankle Pocket

Stretch cotton Lycra knit fabric is a great choice for an ankle pocket. It makes a safe place to store an important key, some money, or a credit card. When you pull a sock up over the pocket, no one can see this secret hiding place for valuables. Knit fabric from The RainShed.

CARRY SMALL VALUABLES IN THIS POCKET WORN AROUND THE ANKLE. IT CAN BE HIDDEN UNDER A SOCK OR WORN OVER THE TOP. COTTON LYCRA STRETCH FABRIC MAKES THE POCKET STRETCH COMFORTABLY AROUND YOUR LEG.

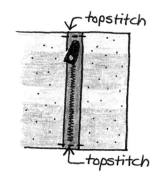

Supplies:

⅛ yd. cotton Lycra stretch fabric
Zipper, 7"
2" piece of Velcro

Steps:

1. Measure around your ankle and add 2" to the measurement. Cut two pieces of fabric 4" wide and the length of the ankle measurement plus 2". (Fig. 1)

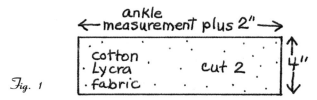

Fig. 1

2. Sew an exposed zipper (see page 10) 1¼" from one end of the right side of one piece of fabric. Cut away the fabric from the back of the zipper teeth and cut off the extra zipper length. (Fig. 2)

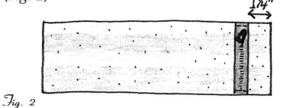

Fig. 2

3. Sew the two fabrics together with right sides facing. Use a ¼" seam allowance and leave an opening for turning the fabrics. (Fig. 3)

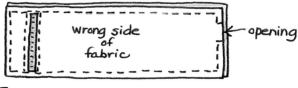

Fig. 3

Clip the corners and trim the seam allowances before turning right side out. Press the edges flat.

4. Topstitch over the zipper ends. (Fig. 4)

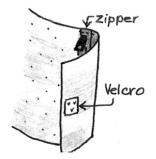

Fig. 4

5. Sew a 1" piece of the hook or rough Velcro on the zipper end of the pocket, centering it on the wrong side of the pocket. (Fig. 5)

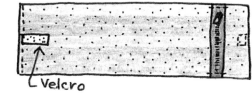

Fig. 5

6. Try the pocket around your ankle and plan the placement of the soft (loop) side of the Velcro. Sew the seam opening closed, then sew on the 2" strip of Velcro. (Fig. 6)

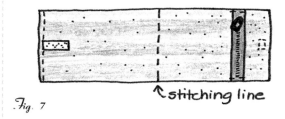

Fig. 6

Add a tie to the zipper head (see page 9).

7. If you wish to make a smaller pocket, sew across the fabrics. (Fig. 7)

Fig. 7

Option: Sew a stretch pocket to wear under a shirt sleeve on your arm.

Wrist Pocket

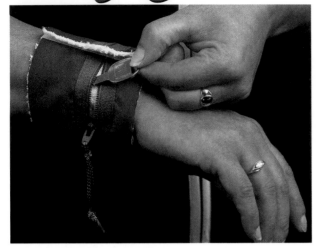

Store small valuables in a pocket worn on your arm. The back layer of the Wrist Pocket is absorbent terrycloth. When you're not wearing the pocket, hang it from the loop tied to the zipper pull.

Supplies:

⅛ yd. lightweight fabric for pocket front
⅛ yd. absorbent fabric for pocket back
Zipper, 12" or longer
3" piece of Velcro
6" cord or narrow ribbon for zipper loop pull

Steps:

1. Measure your wrist and add 4" for the overlap. (For adults, approximately 12", for children, approximately 10"-11".) Cut the pocket fabrics 3½" wide by the length you just measured. (Fig. 1)

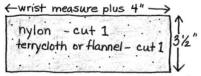

Fig. 1

2. Sew an exposed zipper (see page 10) 1" from the top edge of the pocket front fabric. Cut away the fabric on the back to expose the zipper teeth. (Fig. 2)

Fig. 2

3. Open the zipper a short distance. Pin the pocket fabrics with right sides together. Sew around the edges with a ¼" seam allowance. Clip the corners and trim the seam allowances and turn the pocket right side out through the open zipper. Press.

4. Pin and sew the hook side of the Velcro over the left edge of the pocket front. Sew the loop or soft side of the Velcro to the back right side. (Fig. 3)

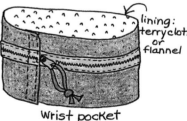

Fig. 3

5. Add a cord loop to the zipper head to make it easy to open the zipper and to hang the wrist pocket on a hook near the door, ready for the next exercise time. (Fig. 4)

Fig. 4

STORE A FEW ESSENTIALS IN A ZIPPER POCKET WORN ON THE WRIST. THIS PROJECT IS A GREAT GIFT FOR A RUNNER OR OUTDOOR EXERCISE ENTHUSIAST WHO WILL APPRECIATE KEEPING A KEY OR MONEY SAFE AND CONVENIENT. CHOOSE NYLON FABRIC AS THE OUTER LAYER AND AN ABSORBENT NATURAL FABRIC SUCH AS TERRYCLOTH, COTTON FLANNEL, OR KNIT AS THE INSIDE LAYER.

Belt Loop Wallet

Slide the loop of this wallet over your belt, then tuck the wallet inside your slacks or skirt. The only visible sign is the loop. You'll appreciate this safe place for a passport, credit cards, or a key.

Supplies:

8½" square of soft, strong fabric
Zipper, 9" or longer
4" length of ribbon or two 1" squares of
  Ultrasuede for grabber tabs
9" length of ¾"-wide ribbon or
  Ultrasuede strip for each belt loop

Steps:

1. On the right side of the 8½" fabric square, sew an exposed zipper (see page 10) 1" from the right edge. Cut the fabric from behind the zipper teeth. Trim away the excess zipper length. (Fig. 1)

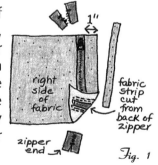

2. Cut the piece of 4" ribbon in half and fold each piece in half. Pin the folded ribbon (or Ultrasuede squares) at the ends of the zippers. Pin one or two loops to the top edge

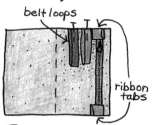

of the bag fabric, as illustrated. (Fig. 2) With two loops you have a choice of colors to match two different belts.

3. Fold the fabric in half towards the zipper with right sides together. Open the zipper a short distance. Pin the three sides together. Sew the raw edges

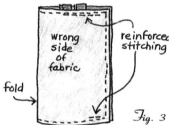

together with a ¼" seam allowance, reinforcing the stitches at the top loop area and at the ends of the zippers. (Fig. 3)

4. Trim the seam allowances and corners with pinking shears and turn the bag right side out. Press the bag and add a tie to the zipper head (see page 9).

Carry valuable property such as your passport, credit cards, and money in this bag. Hidden inside your clothing, this wallet provides secure storage.

Option: When you are not wearing a belt, skirt, or pants, pin the wallet loops inside the garment you are wearing. Consider pinning it to a side seam.

SLIDE THE LOOP OF THIS BAG OVER A BELT AND SLIDE THE WALLET INSIDE YOUR CLOTHING. ONLY THE LOOP IS EXPOSED, AND YOU CAN PLAN THE LOOP TO BLEND WITH THE BELT. MAKE THIS WALLET FOR MEN AND WOMEN. CHOOSE A SOFT BUT STRONG FABRIC SUCH AS NYLON, TENCEL, OR ULTRASUEDE.

Neck Strap Money Holder

Wear a secure wallet around your neck and beneath your clothing. Two zipper pockets hold the essentials for a shopping trip: credit cards, money, and your shopping list. Tencel fabric and ribbon from The RainShed, zippers by A&E.

Supplies:

½ yd. soft yet sturdy fabric
Two zippers, 7"
1 yd. ribbon or cord
Four 1" squares of Ultrasuede for zipper grabber tabs
Cord lock (optional)

Steps:

1. Cut two pieces of fabric for the bag: 5½" x 14½" and 5½" x 4". (Fig. 1)

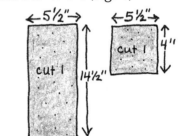

Fig. 1

2. Place one zipper along the top 5½" edge of the smaller piece of fabric with the right sides of the fabric and zipper facing up. With the zipper teeth just above the fabric edge, sew only on the lower side of the zipper tape. Turn under and press ¼" of the other 5½" edge. (Fig. 2)

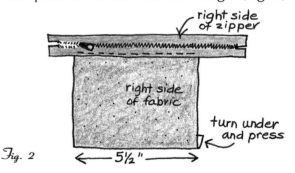

Fig. 2

CARRY CREDIT CARDS, A PASSPORT, MONEY, AND OTHER SMALL VALUABLES IN THIS BAG THAT HANGS AROUND THE NECK AND HIDES BENEATH OUTER CLOTHING. CHOOSE FABRIC SUCH AS A LIGHTWEIGHT NYLON, TENCEL, OR A DURABLE FABRIC THAT WILL BE COMFORTABLE AND SOFT.

3. Sew the top of the zipper 2½" below the top edge of the right side of the larger piece of fabric. Then sew the turned-under hem of the smaller fabric to the larger piece. (Fig. 3)

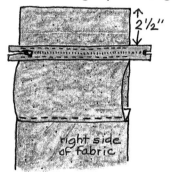

Fig. 3

4. Sew the second zipper ¾" below the top edge of the larger fabric and cut away the fabric from behind the zipper teeth of both zippers. (Fig. 4)

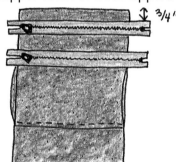

Fig. 4

5. Pin the four grabber tabs over the ends of the zippers (see page 9). Pin the ends of the neck cord at the top edge of the fabric ½" from each side edge. (Fig. 5)

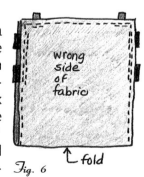

Fig. 5

Open the top zipper a short distance. Fold the fabric piece in half with the right sides of the fabric together and the neck cord tucked inside. Pin the edges and sew with ¼" seam allowances around the three sides, reinforc-

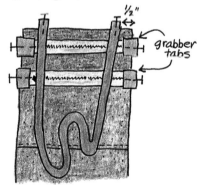

Fig. 6

ing the stitching over the zipper ends and over the ribbon ends. (Fig. 6)

Clip the corners and turn the bag right side out and press. Add ribbons or ties to both zipper heads (see page 9).

6. Slide a cord lock over the loop end of the ribbon so the length of the bag is adjustable. (Fig. 7)

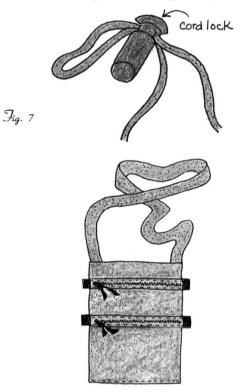

Fig. 7

Option: This bag can be adapted as a "bra stash" bag. (Fig. 8) Natural fiber fabrics such as cotton or silk will be most comfortable to wear next to the skin. Cut the fabrics 4½" wide and sew 8" pieces of ribbon to the bag top sides. Sew narrow pieces of Velcro to the ends of the ribbons, as illustrated.

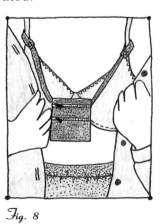

Fig. 8

Five-Zipper Wallet

Five zipper compartments provide separate compartments for money, stamps, credit cards, a comb, and more. Each zipper head has a pull of red Ultrasuede (Sensuede). See the pulls of the two zippers on the back of the bag extending to the right. Nylon fabric from The RainShed.

Supplies:

⅓ yd. soft but sturdy fabric
Five zippers, 9" or longer
4" piece of 1"-wide ribbon
Two 1" x 4" Ultrasuede pieces
18" ribbon or cord for zipper pulls

Steps:

1. Cut three pieces of fabric 8" x 12". (Fig. 1)

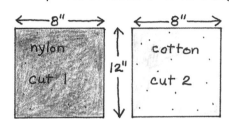

Fig. 1

On the right side of the fabric that will be the top layer, mark the horizontal center line across the 8" side and pin one zipper centered on the line with the zipper pull at the left edge. Measure and mark lines ½" and 2½" above the center zipper. Next, measure and mark lines ¾" and 2¾" below the center zipper. (Fig. 2)

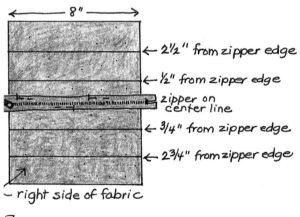

Fig. 2

2. Pin the zippers right side up on the 2½" and 2¾" lines on the fabric. Note the placement of the zipper heads on each side of the fabric (2½" at the right edge; 2¾" at the left edge). Sew around the zippers. (Fig. 3) Cut the fabric away from the back of the zippers.

USE THE FIVE COMPARTMENTS OF THIS WALLET FOR COINS OF DIFFERENT COUNTRIES, STAMPS, PENS, OR OTHER SUPPLIES. CHOOSE NYLON OR OTHER SOFT BUT STRONG FABRICS FOR THIS WALLET. I USED NYLON AS THE OUTER FABRIC AND TWO INNER LAYERS OF LIGHTWEIGHT COTTON.

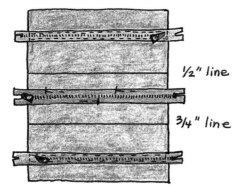

Fig. 3

3. Place and pin the second fabric layer beneath the first layer, with the right side of the fabric facing up. Pin and sew on the zippers along the ½" line (zipper head at the right edge) and the ¾" line (zipper head at the left edge), pinning and sewing through both layers of fabric. (Fig. 4) Cut away the two layers of fabric from the back of the zippers.

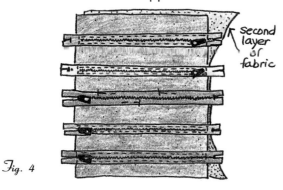

second layer of fabric

Fig. 4

4. Place and pin the third layer of fabric (shown in pink here) on top of the second layer, with the right side of the fabric facing up. (Fig. 5)

Now it's time to sew on the center zipper. First, reduce the zipper bulk in the corners of the wallet by sewing ribbon ends to the zipper, as explained on page 47. (Fig. 6)

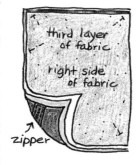

third layer of fabric

right side of fabric

zipper

Fig. 5

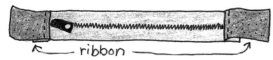

ribbon

Fig. 6

Repin the zipper to the center of the right side of the outer wallet fabric. Sew the zipper with two rows of stitching and cut the three fabric layers from behind the zipper teeth. (Fig. 7)

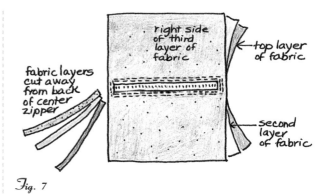

right side of third layer of fabric

top layer of fabric

fabric layers cut away from back of center zipper

second layer of fabric

Fig. 7

5. Trim off the excess lengths of the zippers beyond the edges of the wallet fabric. Place and pin the strips of Ultrasuede (large grabber tabs) over the zipper ends on both sides of the bag. Sew them in place, stitching near

Ultrasuede grabber tabs

Fig. 8

the edge of the fabric, making sure the zipper heads are pulled away from the stitching area. (Fig. 8) Once the bag is sewn together, the strips will serve as zipper tab grabbers on both sides of the bag.

6. Open the center zipper a short distance. Fold the bag in half with right sides together. Pin the edges together and sew around with a ¼" seam allowance. (Fig. 9)

center zipper

wrong side of wallet

Fig. 9

Turn the bag right side out through the center zipper and tie ribbons or strips of Ultrasuede to each of the five zipper pulls (see page 9).

Option: Sew a loop at the side of the bag to hold a key ring. (Fig. 10)

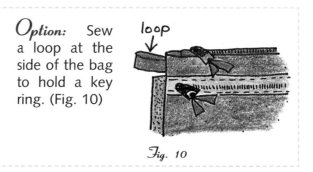

loop

Fig. 10

Hanger Cover

Make hanger covers with zipper pockets for men and women. The white satin cover is made from fabrics and lace left over from sewing a bridal gown; it's a great gift idea for the bride. Storage pockets are added to the bottom edges of the hanger covers and to the front. Purple and teal fabrics from Marcus Brothers Textiles.

WHEN A GARMENT IS PLACED ON THIS HANGER, THE POCKETS BECOME HIDDEN COMPARTMENTS FOR STORING VALUABLE DOCUMENTS SUCH AS AIRLINE TICKETS, PASSPORTS, AND TRAVELER'S CHECK NUMBERS. NECKTIES AND JEWELRY ARE ALSO EASILY STORED IN THE POCKETS. THIS PROJECT IS A PRACTICAL GIFT FOR TRAVELERS AND FOR COLLEGE STUDENTS LIVING IN A DORM ROOM WITH LIMITED PRIVATE SPACE. FABRICS TO SELECT FOR THE HANGER COVER INCLUDE COTTON, LEFTOVER SATIN FROM A BRIDAL GOWN, AND OTHER LIGHT TO MEDIUM WEIGHT FABRICS.

Supplies:

Sturdy hanger, plastic or wood (no wire hangers for this project!)
⅓ yd. light to medium weight fabric
¼ yd. fabric for contrasting fabric pocket
Zippers: 18" or longer for bottom pocket
12" or longer for outside pocket
Small scraps of paper-backed fusible web

Steps:

1. Place the hanger on the wrong side of the fabric chosen for the cover. Trace the top and side edges of the hanger and add 1" to the tracing. (Fig. 1)

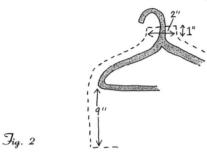

Fig. 1

Mark a 2" opening for the hanger top and add a 1" extension. Extend the outer lines 9" down from the ends of the hanger. (Fig. 2)

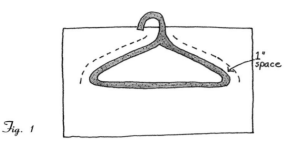

Fig. 2

Cut two pieces of fabric for the hanger cover based on the lines extended beyond the tracing.

2. Sew a pocket with an exposed zipper (see page 10) to one or both sides of the hanger cover, on the right side of the fabric. The purple hanger cover has a pocket made from an 8" x 11" piece of teal fabric with a zipper sewn 1" from the top 11" edge. (Fig. 3)

Turn under all four edges of the fabric ¼" and press. Sew the pocket to one layer of the hanger cover fabric 1¼" from the bottom edge of the fabric. (Fig. 4)

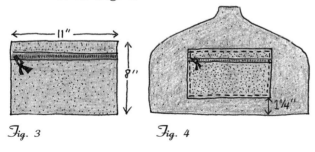

Fig. 3   *Fig. 4*

3. Sew the zipper to the bottom edges of the hanger cover in one of these two ways:

a. Either use the exposed method and sew the zipper over the edges of the fabrics, with the right sides of the fabric edges meeting at the zipper teeth. (Fig. 5)

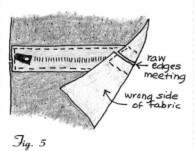

Fig. 5

b. Or turn the fabric edges under ¼" and press them. Then pin and sew the zipper to the back side of the pressed edges. (Fig. 6)

Fig. 6

4. Turn the hanger fabrics wrong sides out. Open the zipper a short distance. Sew with ½" seam allowances up each side of the hanger cover and to 1" below the top of the opening, reinforcing the stitches at the edge of the opening. (Fig. 7)

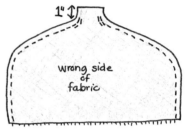

Fig. 7

5. Turn under the fabric at the opening and press it inside the hanger cover. If you want to keep this fabric in place, fuse it to the cover fabric with small pieces of paper-backed fusible web.

6. Turn the cover right side out through the open zipper. Press the edges and add cord or ribbon pulls to the zipper heads (see page 9). Insert the hanger.

Options:

- Omit the outside pocket to make this project even quicker to sew.
- From the photo you'll see that this project is a good one for men and women. You could also sew one for a child. When you select an appropriate print that matches the person's interests or hobbies, this is certain to be a very popular gift.
- See the next project for a jewelry holder addition to the hanger cover.

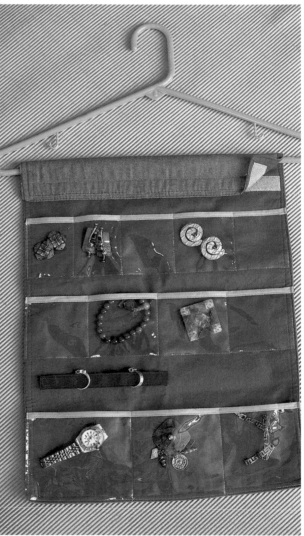

Here's a safe and secure way to carry jewelry while you travel. Select a placemat as the base for this jewelry holder. It wraps around the bottom bar of a hanger with a Velcro closure and then folds up to tuck into the hanger cover. Hanger cover fabrics from Marcus Brothers Textiles.

ADD ANOTHER FEATURE TO THE HANGER COVER ON PAGE 90 WITH THIS FOLD-UP JEWELRY STORAGE BAG. MADE FROM A RECTANGULAR PLACEMAT, THIS CLEVER ORGANIZER WRAPS AROUND THE LOWER HANGER BAR AND ATTACHES WITH A VELCRO CLOSURE. IT'S A SAFE AND HIDDEN WAY TO CARRY JEWELRY.

Supplies:

Rectangular cloth placemat
Plastic or wooden hanger with a bottom
  crossbar (no wire hangers allowed!)
¼ yd. clear vinyl
1½ yd. bias tape binding
13" piece of Velcro
12" length of ⅝"-wide ribbon
Teflon presser foot
Cellophane tape

Steps:

1. Sew a 12" strip of Velcro to the shorter edge of the right side of the placemat. Sew the other half of the Velcro 3½" from the top edge. (Fig. 1)

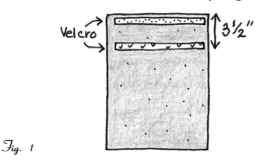

Velcro

3½"

Fig. 1

2. Cut three pieces of vinyl for the pockets. Cut two 3"-wide strips and one 4"-wide strip, all slightly longer than the width of the placemat. (Fig. 2)

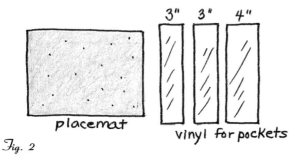

3" 3" 4"

placemat

vinyl for pockets

Fig. 2

3. Sew bias tape binding to one edge of each piece of vinyl.

4. Position the three vinyl pieces on the right side of the placemat. Use tape to hold the bottom edges on the placemat and pin the top corners in place through the bias binding. Sew the sides and bottom edge of each vinyl piece to the placemat and trim away extra vinyl on the sides. Sew divisions in each piece to form smaller pockets. (Fig. 3) It's easiest to sew on vinyl with a Teflon presser foot on the machine.

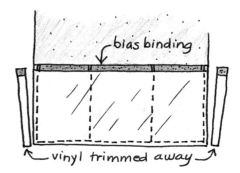

bias binding

vinyl trimmed away

Fig. 3

5. To make the ring holder, fold the 12" ribbon in half and sew the edges together. Cut a small piece of Velcro to sew to the folded end of the ribbon. Sew the other end of the ribbon to the placemat in a space between the rows of pockets. Sew the other half of the Velcro to the placemat beneath the end of the ribbon. (Fig. 4)

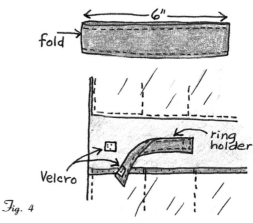

6"

fold

ring holder

Velcro

Fig. 4

6. Attach the jewelry holder to the hanger crossbar and load the pockets with pins, earrings, and necklaces.

Options:

- Use mesh fabric for the pockets instead of vinyl.
- Sew narrow strips of Velcro to the open pocket edges for pockets that close more securely.
- Hang this jewelry holder inside the hanger cover (see page 90), then fold up your valuables and zip them out of sight. (Fig. 5)

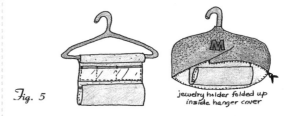

Fig. 5

jewelry holder folded up inside hanger cover

Accessories for the Beach and Beyond

Accessories for the Beach and Beyond provide convenient storage for trips to warm weather locations or an indoor pool.

To all my friends

Pareu: A Swimsuit Cover-Up and More

A simple rectangle of fabric becomes an attractive beach cover-up. The pareu also works as a shawl, ground cover cloth, or a light blanket.

MAKE A PAREU (PRONOUNCED PA-RAY'-OO) TO COORDINATE WITH A BATHING SUIT AND YOU'LL DISCOVER MANY MORE WAYS TO USE IT. A SIMPLE LARGE SQUARE OF CLOTH CAN BE WRAPPED AND TIED ON THE BODY, USED AS A LIGHTWEIGHT BLANKET, A TABLECLOTH, OR TIED TOGETHER AT THE CORNERS FOR CARRYING BEACH TOYS. CHOOSE LIGHTWEIGHT, SOFT, THIN FABRICS SUCH AS RAYON CHALLIS OR CRINKLE COTTONS FOR THE BEST DRAPE WHEN WEARING A PAREU.

Steps:

1. To determine the best size for your pareu, experiment with different sizes of fabric. Use the drawings in Fig. 2 as examples of how to tie and arrange the pareu on your body. Your size and height will help you decide if you need more or less fabric for a beach cover-up. Pre-wash the fabric and cut off the selvage edges.

2. Finish the fabric edges on all four sides. Some fabrics can simply be cut with pinking shears if fraying is not a problem. The red pareu in the photo has a narrow hem turned under twice and sewn. The pareu on the right has rolled edges stitched on the serger. Also consider using ¼" strips of paper-backed fusible web to fuse the fabric edges in place. (Fig. 1)

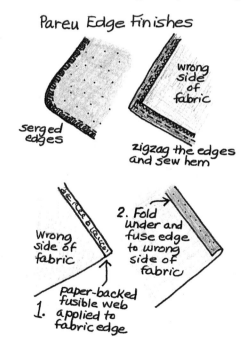

Pareu Edge Finishes

Fig. 1

3. Refer to the illustrations for a variety of ways to tie the pareu. Then invent some of your own. (Fig. 2)

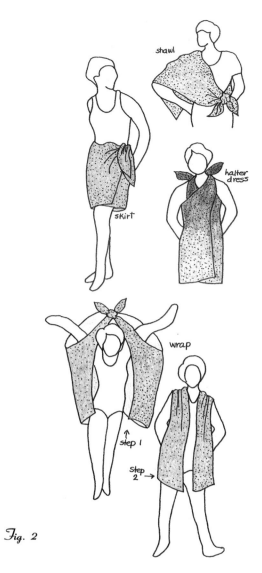

Fig. 2

4. To pack a pareu, fold up and roll the fabric into a tight roll. Hold it in place with a rubber band or bands, or make a Stuff Sack for it (see page 20). Stash it in your carry-on bag.

Options:

- Use the pareu as a shawl during a cool airplane ride or in an air conditioned restaurant.
- Tie opposite corners together and carry beach gear in the pouch that's formed. (Fig. 3)

tie these corners together next

Fig. 3

Beach Towel Carrier

Sew Easy

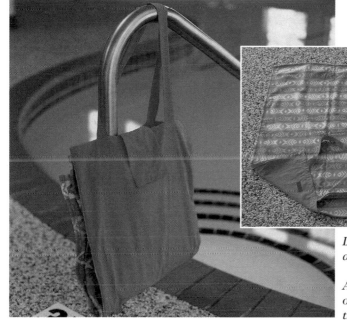

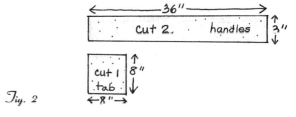

Left. Travel to the pool with a beach towel folded into a tote style carrier. Nylon fabric from The RainShed.

Above. Open the tote, unfold the towel, and spread it on the sand. Stuff another towel or clothing inside the tote section and you'll have a pillow.

Supplies:

Beach towel (mine measures 36" x 70")
¾ yd. lightweight fabric for tote addition
2" piece of Velcro

Steps:

1. Measure across the short end of a beach towel and add 3". Cut a piece of fabric to that measurement by 16" wide. (Fig. 1)

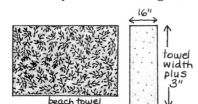

16"

towel width plus 3"

beach towel

Fig. 1

Cut two handles for the tote, each 3" x 36". Also cut an 8" square piece of fabric for the tab closure. (Fig. 2)

36"

Cut 2.   handles   3"

cut 1 tab   8"

8"

Fig. 2

2. On the tote fabric, turn under ¼" and press the long edges. On the short ends, turn under 1½" hems and press. Check the fabric piece on the towel to see if this length fits well. Adjust if necessary and pin and sew the 1½" hems. (Fig. 3)

CARRY THIS COMBINATION TOTE BAG/BEACH TOWEL ON YOUR NEXT TRIP TO THE POOL OR BEACH. THE FULL SIZE BEACH TOWEL FOLDS OVER A NYLON FABRIC BASE WITH HANDLES SO IT IS EASY TO CARRY OVER YOUR SHOULDER. WHEN YOU GET SETTLED ON THE SAND OR A LOUNGE CHAIR, STUFF CLOTHING INSIDE THE TOTE TO MAKE A PILLOW AT THE TOP OF THE BEACH TOWEL. FABRICS SUGGESTED FOR THIS PROJECT INCLUDE NYLON, COTTON, AND LIGHTWEIGHT DENIM.

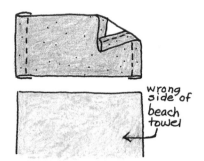

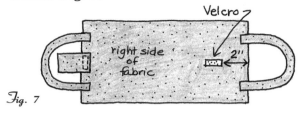

Fig. 3

the soft or loop side of Velcro to the other end of the bag fabric, 2" from the edge and at the center. (Fig. 7)

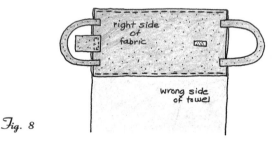

Fig. 7

3. Fold the handle fabrics in half lengthwise with the right sides of the fabric together. Sew with ¼" seam allowances and leave an opening for turning. (Fig. 4)

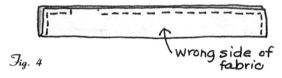

Fig. 4

Turn the handle right side out after clipping and trimming the seam allowances. Sew the ends of each handle piece to the right side of the bag fabric piece, 3" from the side edges. (Fig. 5)

Fig. 5

4. Fold the tab fabric in half with right sides together. Sew ¼" seams around three edges, leaving a small opening for turning. Turn the tab right side out. Sew the 2" strip of the hook or rough side of Velcro vertically at the center of one end of the tab. (Fig. 6)

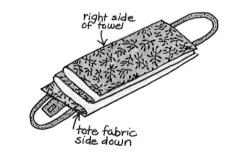

Fig. 6

Sew the other end of the tab to the bag fabric, centered between the handles. Then sew

5. With wrong sides together, pin and sew the two long sides of the bag fabric piece to the towel. (Fig. 8)

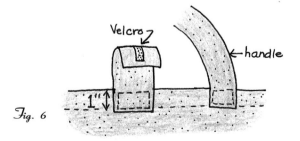

Fig. 8

6. To fold the towel into the tote, place the tote fabric side down and accordion fold the towel over the top of the tote. Then fold the tote fabric in half, bringing the handles together and closing the tab over the top. (Fig. 9)

Fig. 9

Options:

- Carry beach supplies in the open ends of the tote.
- Add a zipper pocket (see page 111) for a small storage place on a corner of the beach towel.
- To hold the tote together on the sides, add tabs with Velcro closures to the long edges of the tote fabric. (Fig. 10)

Fig. 10

Mesh Beach Bag

An "Anything" Pocket on this beach bag holds a bottle of water and other supplies you'll want to keep safe: keys and money. Carry the bag over your shoulder and fill it with everything you'll need for a trip to the beach. Nylon and mesh fabrics from The RainShed.

Supplies:

⅔ yd. mesh fabric
2¼ yd. heavy cord for bag drawstring
¼ yd. nylon fabric for bag bottom, casing, and zipper pocket
Zipper, 7" or 9" for pocket

Steps:

1. Cut a 24" x 36" piece of mesh fabric. Cut a 4" x 36" piece of nylon fabric for the drawstring casing and a 6" x 36" piece of nylon for the bag bottom edge. (Fig. 1)

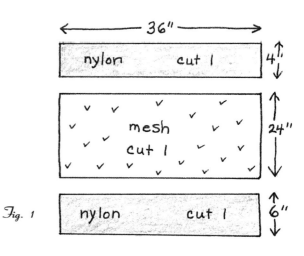

Fig. 1

← 36" →

nylon   cut 1   4"

mesh
cut 1   24"

nylon   cut 1   6"

USE THIS BAG AT THE BEACH OR SEW IT IN OTHER FABRICS FOR A SHOPPING TOTE. IT'S A HANDY BAG TO SLIP OVER YOUR SHOULDER. AN OUTSIDE ZIPPER POCKET IS A GREAT FEATURE FOR STORING KEYS, MONEY, OR SMALL ITEMS THAT COULD GET LOST INSIDE THE BAG. FABRICS FOR THIS PROJECT ARE MESH AND LIGHTWEIGHT RIPSTOP OR SUPPLEX NYLON.

2. On the drawstring casing, turn under ¼" on the short ends and sew. Fold under and press ¼" on the long edges. Then fold and press the casing in half lengthwise with the wrong sides of the fabric together. (Fig. 2)

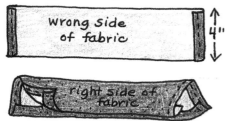

Fig. 2

Sew the casing to the 36" top edge of the mesh fabric. (Fig. 3)

Fig. 3

3. Turn under ¼" and press one 36" edge of the bag bottom fabric. Pin the fabric so its raw edge meets the bottom edge of the mesh fabric and sew the folded edge and the other three edges to the mesh. (Fig. 4)

Fig. 4

4. Use a bodkin or large safety pin to thread the drawstring cord through the casing. Pin the two cord ends to the bottom corner of the right side of the bag. (Fig. 5)

pin cord ends here

Fig. 5

5. Turn the bag wrong side out. Pin together the side and bottom edges of the bag. Make sure the cords are kept out of the seam areas. Sew twice to reinforce the seamlines on the bag sides, bottom, and where the cords are attached. Turn the bag right side out.

6. Try the bag on over your shoulder to determine where a zipper pocket (an "Anything" Bag, see page 11) would work best. The pocket on the bag in the photo was made from two fabric pieces 8" x 12". The exposed zipper (see page 10) was sewn on at an angle and a grabber tab (see page 9) was added at each end of the zipper. (Fig. 6)

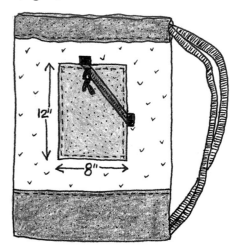

Fig. 6

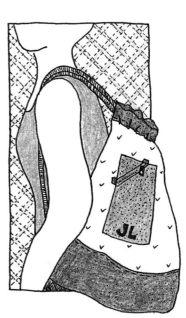

Option: To add a feminine touch to this bag, use lace fabric, either one or two layers, instead of mesh fabric.

Ground Cover Cloth

Sew Easy

Above. Set up a comfortable spot for a picnic with a flannel and nylon ground cover cloth. Fabric straps in the corners of the cloth loop around tent pegs to secure the cloth. Bandanna handkerchiefs make great picnic napkins, and hospitality gifts (see page 113). Don't forget to invite your favorite teddy bear! Nylon fabric from The RainShed.

Left. When the picnic is over, store the ground cover cloth by folding and inserting it in the pocket sewn to the back of the cloth.

STORE THIS FLANNEL AND NYLON GROUND COVER IN THE TRUNK OF THE CAR OR WITH THE CAMPING GEAR. SPREAD OUT ON THE GRASS OR SAND AND ANCHORED WITH TENT PEGS, IT SETS THE SCENE FOR A GREAT PICNIC. WATER-REPELLENT NYLON IS SUGGESTED FOR THE BOTTOM OF THE COVER CLOTH AND COTTON FLANNEL IS A COMFORTABLE TOP FABRIC.

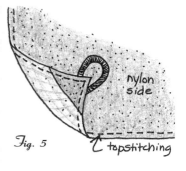

Supplies:

2 yd. nylon fabric, 60" wide
60" flannel fabric, 60" wide
20" heavy cord or webbing for corner ties
Four tent pegs

Steps:

1. Cut both the nylon and flannel fabrics into 60" squares. Cut four 4" squares of nylon fabric. Cut the storage pocket piece 16" x 12". (Fig. 1)

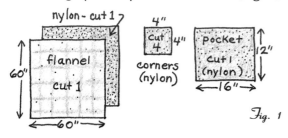

Fig. 1

2. Fold the small squares in half on the diagonal with the wrong sides of the fabric together, and pin and sew each one in a corner of the right side of the flannel fabric. (Fig. 2)

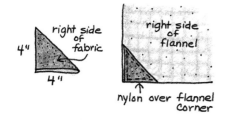

Fig. 2

3. Cut four 5" pieces of cord or webbing. Pin and sew the cords to each corner, stitching back and forth to reinforce the seams. (Fig. 3)

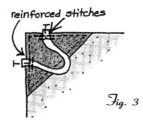

Fig. 3

4. Pin the right side of the nylon fabric to the right side of the flannel. Sew around the edges with the nylon side up. Leave an 8"-9" opening to turn the fabrics right side out. (Fig. 4)

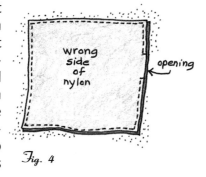

Fig. 4

5. Clip the edges and trim the corners, or use pinking shears for trimming. Press the seamlines and turn the cover right side out. Sew the opening closed. Press the edges and sew ¼" from the edge to topstitch the two fabric layers together. Again, sew with the nylon side up. (Fig. 5)

Fig. 5

6. Turn under twice and sew the four sides of the pocket fabric. Place and pin one of the longer (16") edges of the pocket to the center of one edge of the cloth on the nylon side. Stitch around the three sides of the fabric to make it a pocket with the open end lined up with the edge of the cover cloth. Sew back and forth at the corners for a strong seam. (Fig. 6)

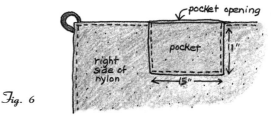

Fig. 6

7. To store the ground cover cloth in the pocket, place the pocket side down and fold up the cloth on the sides to line up with the pocket edges. Turn the cover over so the pocket is up and fold the other end of the cloth toward the pocket and tuck it inside. Don't forget to tuck the tent pegs inside the pocket.

Options:

- Make grommet holes in place of cord loops in the reinforced corners of the cloth.
- Use this cloth in the car trunk when you need to transport messy cargo. Place the nylon side up for an easier-to-clean surface.
- Add a handle or handles to the storage pocket, or a strap with Velcro so the cloth can be rolled up. (Fig. 7)

Fig. 7

Traveling Kits

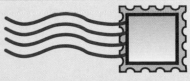

Traveling Kits hold valu-
able supplies for daily needs
and emergencies. Sew these
clever bags and fill them
with the items suggested.

To all my friends

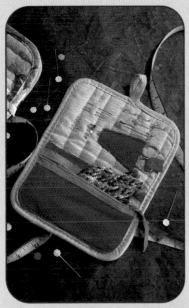

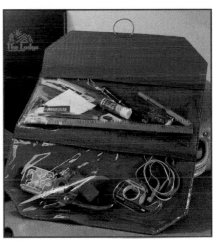

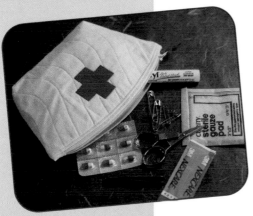

First-Aid Kit

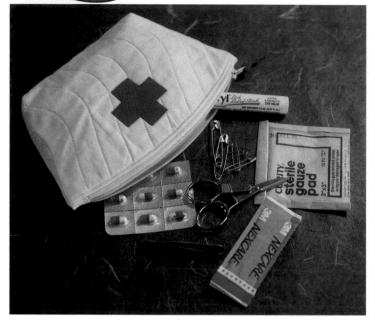

Use the international red cross symbol of first aid to trim a small size Bedside Bag for a first aid kit.

Steps:

1. Refer to the instructions for the medium size Bedside Bag on page 46.

2. To applique the cross, you'll need a scrap of red fabric and some paper-backed fusible web. Trace the appliqué design from page 128 on a piece of paper-backed fusible web. Follow the manufacturer's instructions for the iron temperature and amount of fusing time needed, and fuse the design to the wrong side of the red applique fabric you've chosen. Cut out the design and peel the paper off the back. Fuse the design to the front of the first-aid bag. Sew

around the edges with a satin applique stitch or a blanket stitch. (Fig. 1)

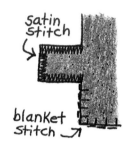

Fig. 1

ITEMS TO INCLUDE IN A FIRST-AID KIT:

bandages
safety pins
aspirin, ibuprofen, or acetominophen
sting relief pads or applicator
antihistamine
adhesive tape
cotton swabs
moleskin
tweezers
antibiotic ointment
first-aid handbook
rubber gloves
scissors
collapsible drinking cup
needle for blisters and slivers

A COMPACT BAG WITH THE RED CROSS SYMBOL OF FIRST AID IS EASILY IDENTIFIABLE IN A SUITCASE, THE GLOVE COMPARTMENT OF A CAR, OR A CUPBOARD IN A RECREATIONAL VEHICLE. THIS BAG IS A MEDIUM SIZE BEDSIDE BAG BUT YOU CAN USE THE SMALL OR LARGE SIZES OF THE SAME BAG IF THEY WOULD WORK BETTER FOR YOU. (THIS IS THE ADVANTAGE OF SEWING: ADAPTING AN IDEA AND PERSONALIZING THE PROJECTS TO FIT OUR NEEDS!)

Potholder Sewing Kit

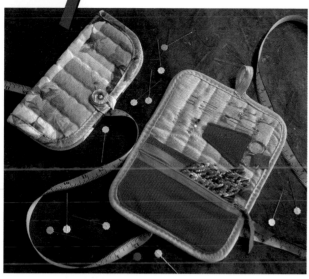

Turn a potholder into a sewing kit with the addition of an inside zipper pocket and a scissors holder. The Thread Braid by Dritz is a practical, compact way to add a thread selection to the sewing kit. Fold the potholder in half and add a button to close the kit.

Supplies:
9" x 7" potholder with loop in center of
  one side
¼ yd. coordinating fabric
Button
4" ribbon for scissors holder
½" piece of Velcro

Steps:

1. Fold the potholder in half along the 9" edge and draw a line across the center.

2. Trace the bottom half (opposite the end with the loop) of the potholder.

3. Sew an "Anything" Bag (see page 11) to fit in the space. Sew the bag edges to the wrong side of the potholder, leaving the top edge open so the bag forms an open pocket for extra storage. (Fig. 1)

Fig. 1

4. Trace the Scissors Holder pattern from page 128. Cut one from a non-fray fabric like felt or Ultrasuede or cut two from fabric. Sew the two fabric layers together, right sides facing, leaving an opening. Turn the holder right side out. Place the holder above the "Anything" Bag with the wide edge closest to the potholder edge and sew along the two long sides. Slide in the scissors. (Fig. 2)

Fig. 2

5. Sew a piece of ribbon to the edge of the potholder nearest to the wide edge of the scissors holder, and sew a small piece of Velcro to the ribbon close to the stitching. Sew the matching Velcro to the loose end of the ribbon. (Fig. 3)

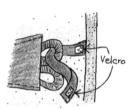

Fig. 3

Loop the ribbon around the scissors handle to hold it in place.

6. Sew a button to the outside of the potholder so the potholder loop can be used to close the sewing kit.

ITEMS TO STORE IN THE SEWING KIT:

needles and thread · buttons
needle threader · thread snag puller
straight and safety pins · paper-backed
scissors · fusible web strips

COLLECT THE BASIC SUPPLIES FOR SEWING AND ADD THEM TO A POTHOLDER! THIS QUICK-TO-MAKE KIT IS A PERFECT GIFT FOR A COLLEGE STUDENT OR SOMEONE MOVING INTO THEIR FIRST APARTMENT. WHEN MOM'S NOT CLOSE BY TO FIX RIPS OR SEW BUTTONS, THIS COLLECTION OF SUPPLIES WILL COME TO THE RESCUE.

Bride's Rescue Kit

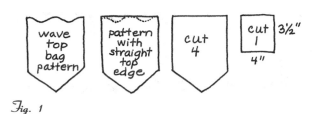

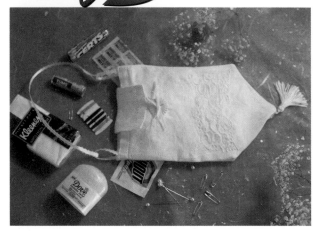

Collect emergency supplies for the bride and stash them in this version of the Wave Top Bag (page 18). She'll appreciate your thoughtfulness when a safety pin is needed by one of the bridesmaids. Encourage the bride to share the bag with other brides on their wedding days.

Supplies:

⅓ yd. soft fabric
24" length of narrow ribbon
Tassel and lace trims (optional)
Button

Steps:

1. Trace the larger size Wave Top Bag pattern from page 117 and draw a straight line across the wavy top. Cut four pieces of fabric from the pattern. Cut a 3½" x 4" piece of fabric for the tab closure. (Fig. 1)

Fig. 1

2. Sew trim to the fabric piece that will be the front of the bag. With the right sides of two bag pieces facing, sew with ¼" seam allowances from the top edges to the pointed ends. Sew the second set of fabric pieces together in the same way and press the seams. (Fig. 2)

Fig. 2

3. Pin a tassel to the right side of one pair of the bag fabrics. (Fig. 3)

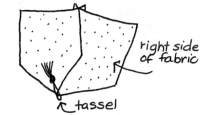

Fig. 3

THE SUPPLIES IN THIS BAG WILL SAVE THE DAY FOR EMERGENCIES WHILE THE BRIDE AND BRIDESMAIDS ARE PREPARING FOR THE WEDDING. MAKE THE BAG FROM AN HEIRLOOM FAMILY FABRIC, OR USE PIECES FROM A STAINED DAMASK TABLECLOTH, AS I DID, AND ADD SPECIAL PIECES OF LACE, POSSIBLY LEFT OVER FROM SEWING THE BRIDAL GOWN. PASS THIS KIT ON TO ALL THE BRIDES IN THE FAMILY, MAKING SURE IT'S ALWAYS FILLED WITH SPOT REMOVER, SAFETY PINS, BREATH MINTS, AND THE OTHER ITEMS ON THE LIST ON PAGE 107. THE BAG IS MADE FROM THE WAVE TOP PATTERN (LARGER SIZE) FOUND ON PAGE 117.

Pin together and sew the two pairs together with the tassel inside. (Fig. 4)

Press the seams and turn the bag right side out. (On the bag in the photo, I used the hemstitched tablecloth edge at the top of the bag so no hemming was required. If your bag top has raw edges, turn them under twice and sew around the top.)

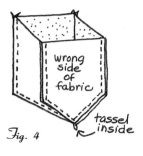

Fig. 4

4. Press the bag with the two center sections folded. Sew darts through the folded edges inside the bag to keep the bag shape, as illustrated. (Fig. 5)

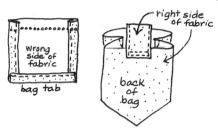

Fig. 5

5. Turn under twice and sew the 4" edges of the tab fabric. Fold under and press one or both 3½" edges. (On the bag in the photo, I used the finished, hemstitched edge of the tablecloth as the finished edge of the tab.) Pin and sew one edge in place on the back of the bag. (Fig. 6)

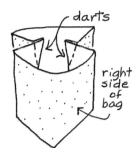

Fig. 6

6. Sew a ribbon loop on the right side of the tab at the open end. Safety pin a 6" piece of ribbon to the bag front, with the pin on the

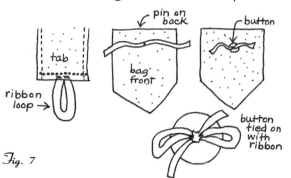

Fig. 7

inside of the bag. Pull the ribbon ends through the holes in a button and tie a bow to hold the button in place. (Fig. 7)

7. On both sides of the bag, sew a 2" strip of ribbon into a loop from one bag corner to another, as illustrated. (Fig. 8)

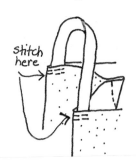

Fig. 8

Cut a 14" piece of ribbon for the bag handle and wrap the ends around the two loops sewn to the bag corners. Sew the ends of the ribbons to the handle. (Fig. 9)

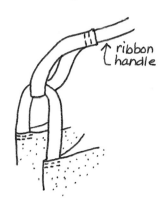

Fig. 9

ITEMS TO INCLUDE IN THE BRIDE'S RESCUE KIT:

small sewing kit
safety pins
aspirin
breath mints
throat lozenges
antacid tablets
sanitary napkins/mini pads/tampons
deodorant
facial tissues
bandages
spot remover packets

Comfort Kit

Fill the Comfort Kit with little luxuries for your hotel home away from home. Luxuries featured here are a lavender aromatherapy bag, scented candle, tea bag, clothespin for holding window draperies closed, and a night light. The bag used for this project is the Easy Napkin Petal Pouch on page 26.

The bag for this kit is the Easy Napkin Petal Pouch (see page 26). I chose a solid color dinner napkin for the bag. Instead of using a double drawstring cord, I cut one piece of satin cord 22" long and used a cord lock to hold the bag closed. To personalize the bag, sew a monogram on one of the corner "petals" of the bag.

One of the items in the bag is a Lavender Scent Bag. Start with two 4" x 6" pieces of cotton fabric and sew them together on three sides with the right sides of the fabrics facing. Pour in ¼ cup of dried lavender and sew the fourth side closed. (Fig. 1)

I also stitched a ribbon to the end of the bag. Place this bag on the pillow before you go to sleep to add a calming scent to the pillowcase.

Fig. 1

OTHER ITEMS TO INCLUDE IN THE COMFORT KIT:

scented candle in a covered tin
clothespin to keep curtains closed or for
    hanging one piece of laundry!
wrapped pieces of fine quality chocolate
scented spray for pillows and bed linens
bubble bath   night light
perfumed soap   calming herb tea
moisturizer   flat rubber sink stopper

FOR A TRAVELER, A COLLECTION OF SPECIAL TREATS AND PLEASANT SCENTS CAN MAKE A HOTEL ROOM A SPA EXPERIENCE. BE NICE TO YOURSELF OR A FRIEND BY MAKING THIS BAG AND FILLING IT WITH SURPRISES AND COMFORT SUPPLIES.

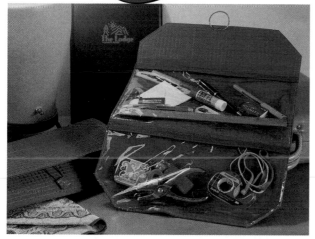

Two pleated vinyl pockets sewn to a placemat hold the supplies you'll need for an office on the road.

Supplies:

Cloth placemat	Teflon presser foot
⅓ yd. vinyl	for sewing machine
28" bias binding	Button
12" piece of ¾"	Ponytail elastic
Velcro	

Steps:

1. Fold the placemat in thirds to determine where the folds will be and draw lines for placing the top edges of the pockets on the wrong side of the placemat. The top edge of the first pocket on my kit is placed at 4" from the placemat top (short edge) and the second pocket is 12" from the top. (Fig. 1)

Cut one piece of vinyl 10" x 14" for the upper pocket and another 8½" x 14" for the lower pocket.

2. Sew bias binding to one 14" edge of each piece of vinyl. Also cut the 12" Velcro piece in half lengthwise and sew the hook or rough side to the wrong side of the bias binding on both pockets. Pin and sew the loop or soft side of the Velcro to the placemat right below the lines drawn on for the top edges of the pockets. (Fig. 1)

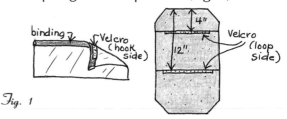
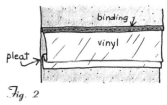

Fig. 1

3. Attach the top edges of the pockets to the Velcro sewn to the placemat. Fold the bottom of the vinyl into a pleat and tape or pin the vinyl to the placemat. (Fig. 2)

Fig. 2

4. Sew around the three sides of each pocket and trim off any extra vinyl that extends beyond the edges of the placemat.

5. Sew the ponytail elastic to the top edge of the placemat by zigzag stitching over the elastic. Sew a button to the opposite side of the placemat to complete the closure. (Fig. 3)

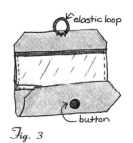

Fig. 3

ITEMS TO STORE IN THE OFFICE KIT:

stapler and staples	calculator
rubber bands	sticky notes
pens	highlighter
eraser	ruler
scissors	business cards
tape	paper clips

CARRY OFFICE SUPPLIES WITH YOU AND FIND THEM QUICKLY IN THIS KIT MADE FROM A PLACEMAT AND FEATURING CLEAR VINYL POCKETS. THE PLACEMAT BAG FOLDS IN THIRDS AND THE CLOSURE IS A PONYTAIL ELASTIC THAT LOOPS AROUND A BUTTON SEWN TO THE PLACEMAT.

Car Kit

A large "Anything" Bag for the car trunk holds jumper cables, gloves, and other emergency supplies. The vinyl pocket on the front of the bag holds the instructions for using the jumper cables. Tapestry fabric from The RainShed.

Supplies:

1 yd. sturdy fabric
½ yd. nylon webbing
Zipper, 18" or longer
¼ yd. vinyl (optional)

Steps:

1. Start with two 18" squares of fabric. Sew an exposed zipper (see page 10) 2" from the top edge of one square. (Fig. 1)

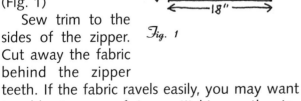

Fig. 1

Sew trim to the sides of the zipper. Cut away the fabric behind the zipper teeth. If the fabric ravels easily, you may want to add extra rows of zigzag stitching on the zipper tape or decorative trim.

2. Cut 18" of webbing for a bag handle. Place the ends 5½" from the sides of the bag and pin them to the top edge.

3. Pin zipper grabber tabs (page 9) over the ends of the zippers. (Fig. 2)

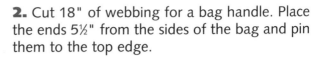

Fig. 2

Open the zipper a short distance and place the two squares of fabric together with right sides meeting. Sew around the squares with a ¼" seam allowance and reinforce the stitching over the handle and zipper ends. Clip the corners and turn the fabrics right sides out.

Option: A special feature that can be added to this bag is the vinyl pocket on the front. Use it to hold the directions for using jumper cables. I photocopied and enlarged the instructions that were printed in small print on the box in which the cables were packaged. Cut a piece of vinyl slightly larger than the instruction information and sew three sides to the bag. (Fig. 3) Slide the instructions into the pocket.

Fig. 3

ITEMS TO STORE IN THE CAR KIT:

jumper cables	tools
ice scraper	non-perishable
umbrella	food items
survival blanket	bandanna or
paper towels	stocking cap
reflector triangle	jack knife
work gloves	flares

KEEP EMERGENCY GEAR FOR YOUR CAR IN AN "ANYTHING" BAG IN THE TRUNK. I CHOSE TAPESTRY FABRIC FOR A CLASSY TOUCH — OTHER VERY STURDY FABRICS SUCH AS CANVAS, DENIM, UPHOLSTERY FABRICS, AND CORDURA NYLON WILL WORK WELL ALSO.

Adapting Clothing for Travel Safety and Comfort

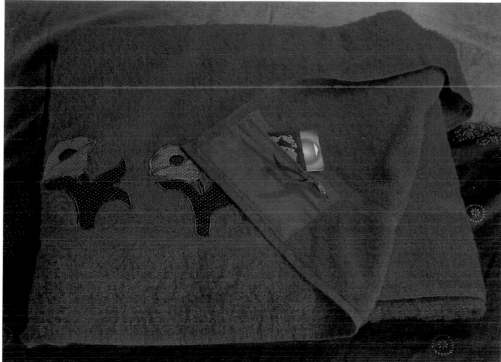

For your trips to the beach or pool, add a corner pocket to a beach towel for a handy storage place. To make the pocket less noticeable so it blends into the towel, choose fabric to match the towel. Make the pocket large enough to hold the supplies you want to store, such as eyeglasses, money, keys, or credit cards. This feature is quick to sew and adds a nice surprise to a towel you give as a gift.

Make a storage bag for a travel robe. Choose a robe that is made of thin fabric so it won't take much space in a suitcase. Fold the robe up into a small square or roll it up and hold it in place with rubber bands. Measure the square or roll and make a Stuff Sack (page 20) of that size. Store the robe in the bag with all your travel supplies and it will be easy to add to your suitcase every time you pack.

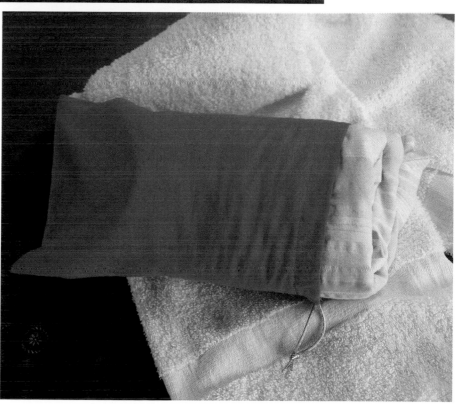

Sew a lace pocket to the bottom edge of a slip for a hidden storage pocket. The lace adds no weight or stiffness to the slip. Use Velcro or a zipper for the top closure of the pocket. Consider the location of the pocket before sewing it to the slip. It may be more comfortable to wear the slip with the pocket on the sides rather than the back or front.

Sew extra pockets inside jackets and other clothing. This pocket was sewn to the seam allowances inside the unlined jacket and is large enough to hold airline tickets or a passport. The fabric print blends with the jacket fabrics and provides hidden storage.

Extend the pockets of a skirt, dress, or pants. Cut off the bottom edges of the pocket and sew on a fabric extension. The enlarged pocket provides a deeper storage place with less chance for valuables like a passport sliding out of the pocket.

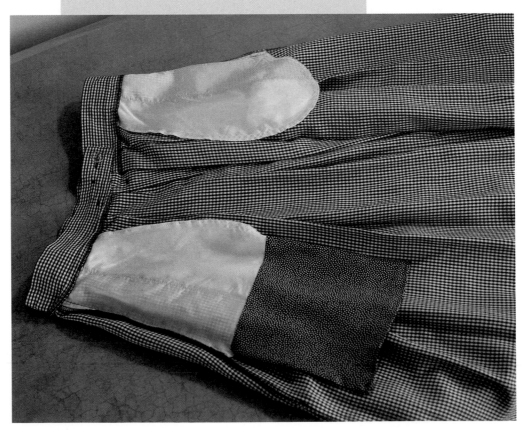

Hospitality Gifts

Clockwise from left to right: Small flags and items such as pens that have your country's flag printed on them represent your home and are well received by residents of other countries. Bandannas are an American invention and a unique gift suggestion. They can be used as scarves, handkerchiefs, or dinner napkins. Kitchen towels are easy to decorate with a band of fabric across one end, or an embroidery or applique design. Pillowcases sewn from conversational cotton prints are another interesting gift. If you know the hobbies of your relatives or foreign hosts, look for printed fabrics that relate to those interests. Instead of wrapping the pillowcases in gift wrap paper, roll them up and tie them with wire-edge ribbon which you can straighten out and re-tie after taking the pillowcase roll out of your suitcase. Small pins representing your hometown, state, or country are compact gifts that are often collected and appreciated by residents of other countries. (You might consider starting your own collection of pins from your travels, and display them on a wide ribbon to hang on the wall.) Tape a variety of postage stamps on an index card for another clever gift idea. Slide the card into a plastic recipe card holder to protect the stamps. If you're not sure how many hospitality gifts you'll need, it's a good suggestion to put together a number of cards with stamps on them. Then, if you don't give them away on your trip, you can use the stamps at home.

WHAT ARE HOSPITALITY GIFTS? THEY ARE GIFTS EASY TO PACK, COMPACT, AND READY TO PRESENT TO NEW FRIENDS, HOSTS FOR HOME VISITS, AND FELLOW TRAVELERS. IT'S OFTEN A CHALLENGE TO FIND NEW GIFT IDEAS, SO THIS PHOTO INCLUDES A VARIETY.

Embellishment Ideas

The hanger cover features a small fabric patch framed with strips of quick fuse bias tape. Initials personalize a Half-Circle Bag. A shoe applique labels another Half-Circle Bag as a shoeshine kit. The Simple Round Bag is decorated with a button monogram. Draw a letter or letters on the bag and sew buttons along the lines. It's a simple idea made interesting by the shapes, colors, and dimensions of the buttons.

TRAVEL ACCESSORIES ARE PERFECT BLANK CANVASES TO DECORATE WITH A VARIETY OF EMBELLISHMENTS. MONOGRAM INITIALS ARE A PERFECT WAY TO PERSONALIZE ANY ACCESSORY. USE THE ALPHABET ON PAGE 116 OR AN ALPHABET FROM ONE OF MY OTHER BOOKS (SEE RESOURCES ON PAGE 128) TO ADD ONE, TWO, OR THREE INITIALS TO TOTES, BAGS, AND HANGER COVERS. APPLIQUES FROM THIS BOOK, OR MY OTHER BOOKS, ARE ANOTHER DECORATING SUGGESTION.

About the Author

Made for Travel is the latest in the series of creative sewing books by teacher and author Mary Mulari. Making travel accessories is one of Mary's favorite projects, along with inventing new ways to embellish plain clothing.

Mary writes and sews at her home in Aurora, Minnesota. She also travels extensively to present sewing seminars across the U.S. She is a frequent guest on PBS television's "Sewing with Nancy" and has taped, with Nancy Zieman, a program based on the projects in this book. Mary's appliqué designs appear on appliqué/embroidery cards she has designed for Husqvarna Viking, Cactus Punch, and Amazing Designs.

Readers of this book are welcome to contact Mary Mulari. See page 128 for contact information.

All the photos in the book were taken at The Lodge at Giants Ridge, a golf and ski resort in northern Minnesota nestled among the pines of the Superior National Forest. (Call toll free 877-442-6877 or visit their website, www.thelodgeatgiantsridge.com.)

The Author Reports on Writing Made for Travel

I discovered my love for sewing, writing, and talking about travel accessories in 1993. Since then, my garment embellishment seminars have been sparked with an extra feature as my students and readers shared my enthusiasm for sewing these down-to-earth accessories in stylish fabrics and scraps left over from other sewing projects. When it was time to update, revise, and add more great ideas to my original book, *Travel Gear & Gifts to Make,* I couldn't wait to sign the contract with Krause Publications to write *Made for Travel.*

The past three summers have found me busy sewing and writing and drawing illustrations for books. I've come to think of the books as my summer job. The month of June was spent at the sewing machine testing the projects and ideas I had in my head. This year almost everything turned out, and no projects were disasters. Well, there was that first try on the Five-Zipper Wallet...

On a few hot days, I just couldn't sit inside at my computer, so I took my writing tablets to the public landing on Wynne Lake to sit by the water and write. The instructions for the cell phone case were written there, while I sat on the dock soaking my feet in the lake. Later, I took two days off to spend time with my college room-mates Diane and Viv, and we explored the lake in rented kayaks. You'll see those kayaks in the picture of the Stuff Sacks on page 20.

All the pictures for the book were taken at The Lodge at Giants Ridge. The photographer Don Hoffman and I took advantage of many areas and rooms at the resort and also the Northern Lights Sports rental shop. The pan of Rice Krispie bars in the fabric tray was one of the first things Don photographed; by the second day of photography, we had eaten the entire contents of the pan.

I look forward to published copies of *Made for Travel.* I know my seminar audiences will be excited about these projects, and I hope you are too. Please contact me if you'd like to share the details of the projects you've made and the innovations you developed. You can write to me at Mary's Productions, Box K-4, Aurora, MN 55705 or by email: mary@marymulari.com

Happy travels and stitches to you!

ABCDEF
GHIJKLM
NOPQR
STUVW
XYZ

Alphabet is printed backwards for ease in tracing onto paper-backed fusible web.

Add the "flourishes" above or below a monogram for extra trim.

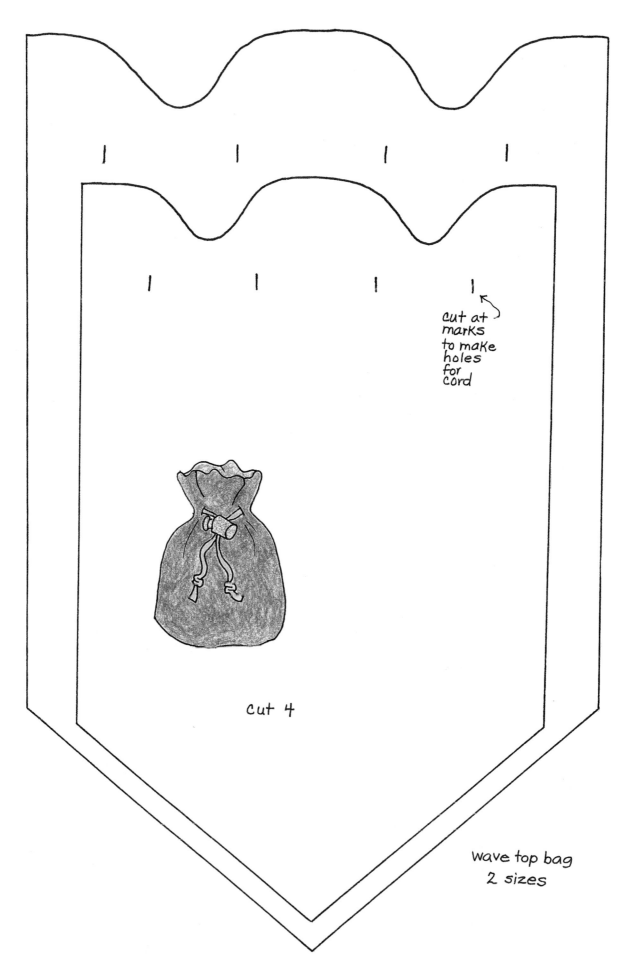

cut at
marks
to make
holes
for
cord

cut 4

wave top bag
2 sizes

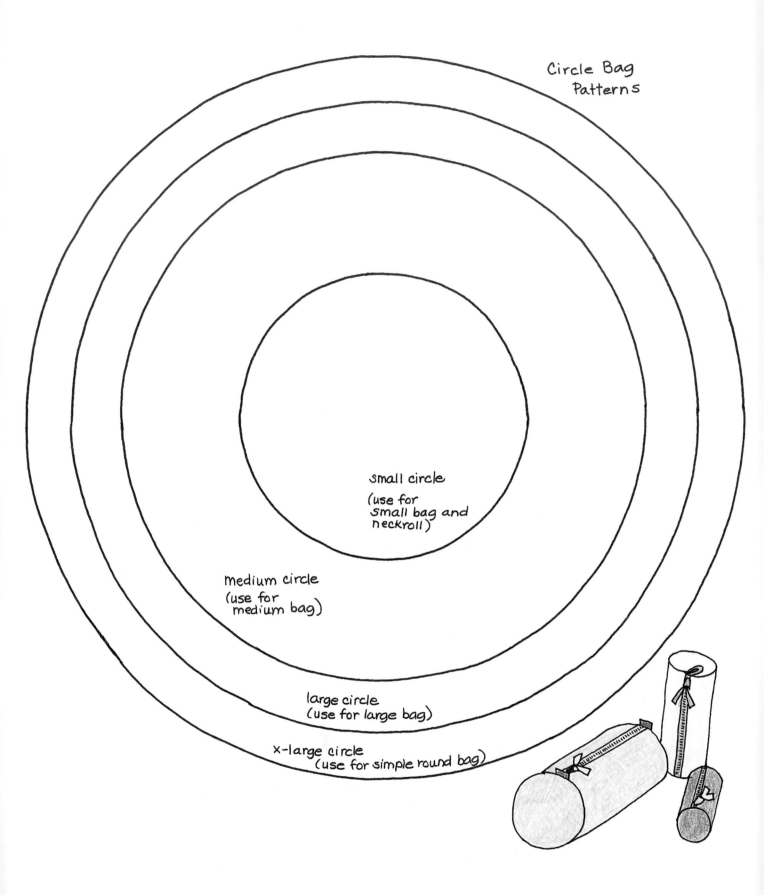

Circle Bag
Patterns

small circle

(use for
small bag and
neckroll)

medium circle
(use for
medium bag)

large circle
(use for large bag)

x-large circle
(use for simple round bag)

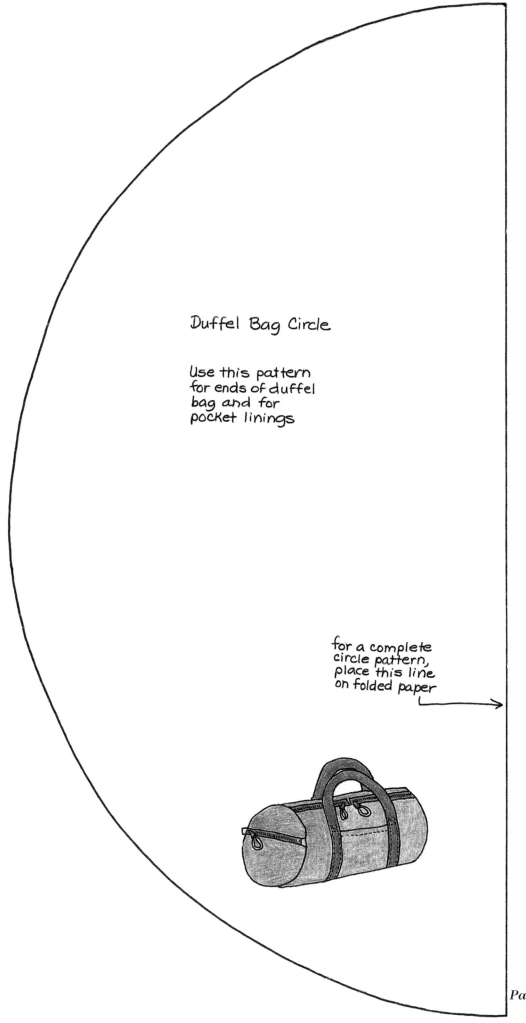

Duffel Bag Circle

Use this pattern
for ends of duffel
bag and for
pocket linings

for a complete
circle pattern,
place this line
on folded paper

Circle Patterns for Drawstring Jewelry Bag

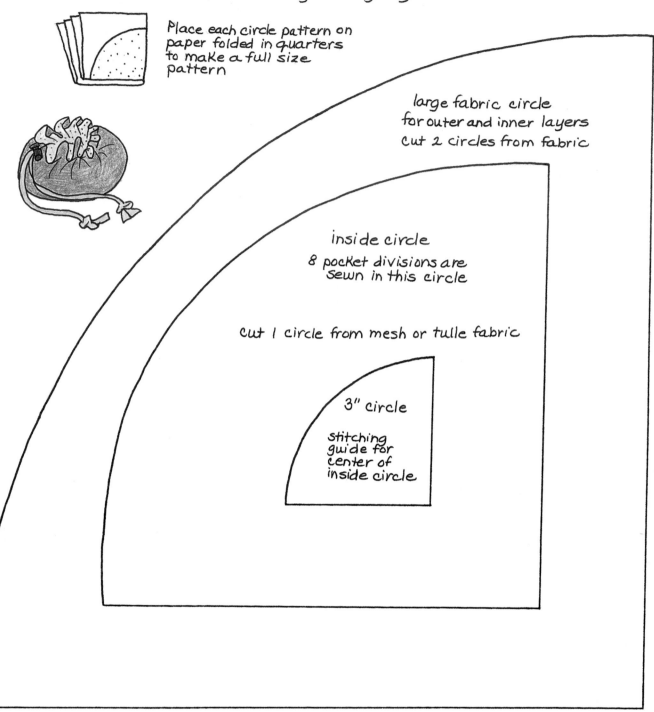

Place each circle pattern on paper folded in quarters to make a full size pattern

large fabric circle
for outer and inner layers
Cut 2 circles from fabric

inside circle

8 pocket divisions are sewn in this circle

Cut 1 circle from mesh or tulle fabric

3" circle

stitching guide for center of inside circle

Bike Bag

Piece C

Meet this edge
to Piece A
←

How to fit pattern
pieces together:

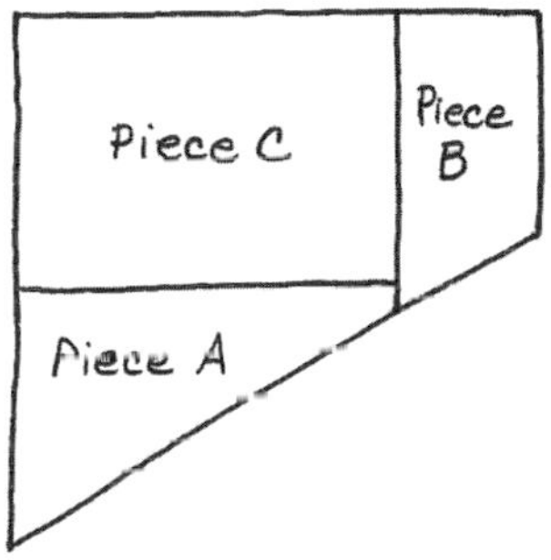

Piece C | Piece B

Piece A

Meet this edge
to Piece B

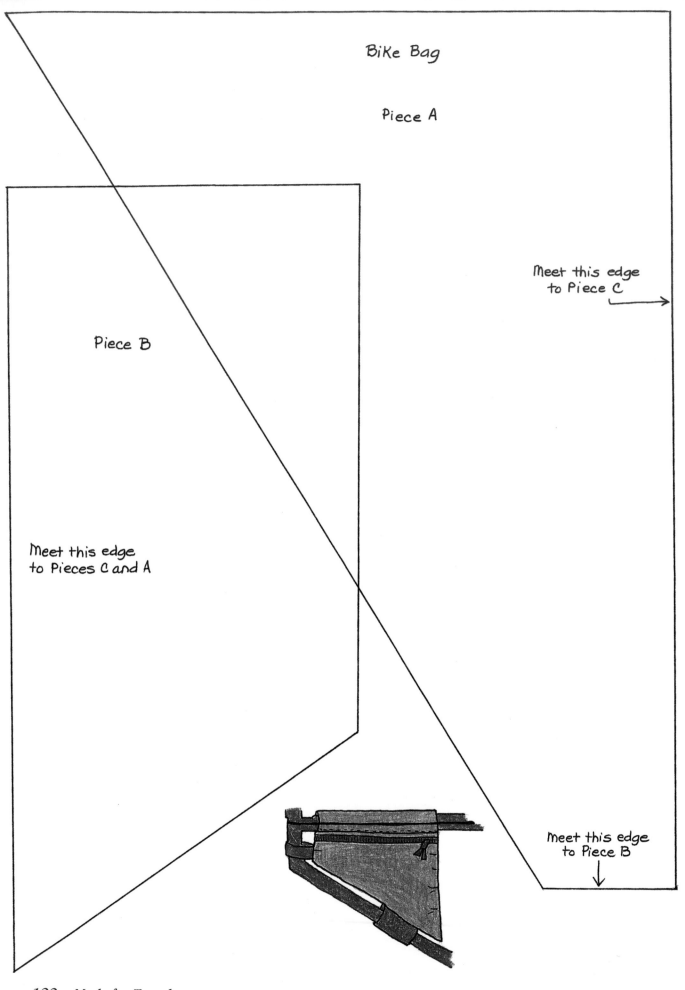

Bike Bag

Piece A

Piece B

Meet this edge
to Piece C →

Meet this edge
to Pieces C and A

Meet this edge
to Piece B
↓

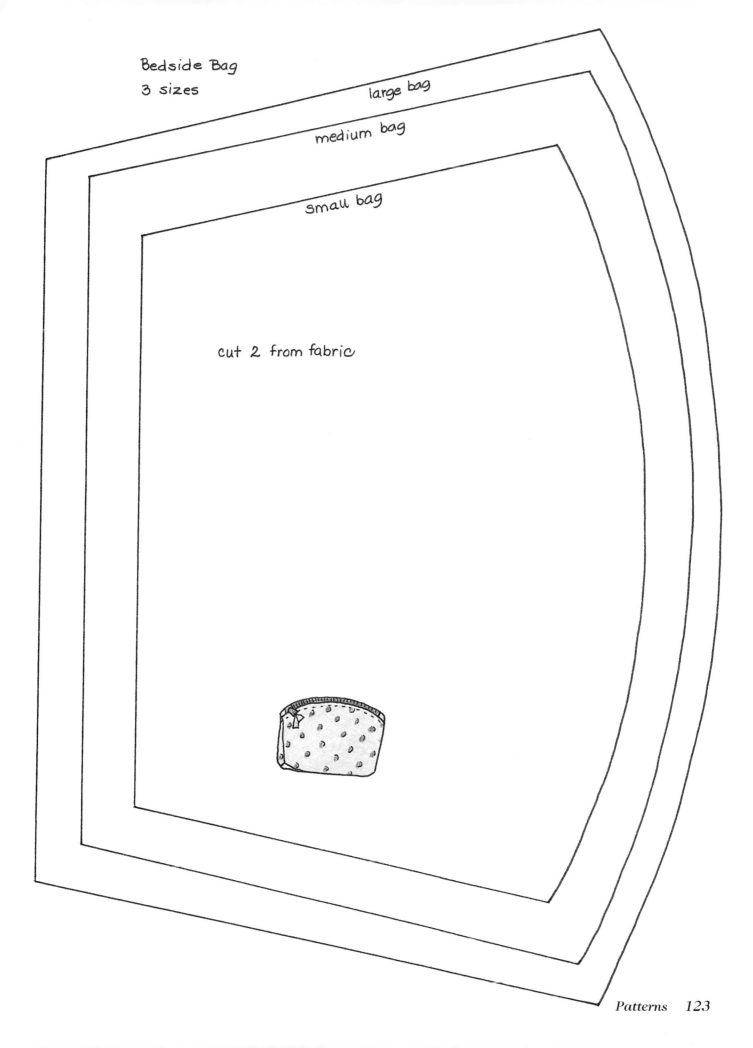

Bedside Bag
3 sizes

large bag

medium bag

small bag

cut 2 from fabric

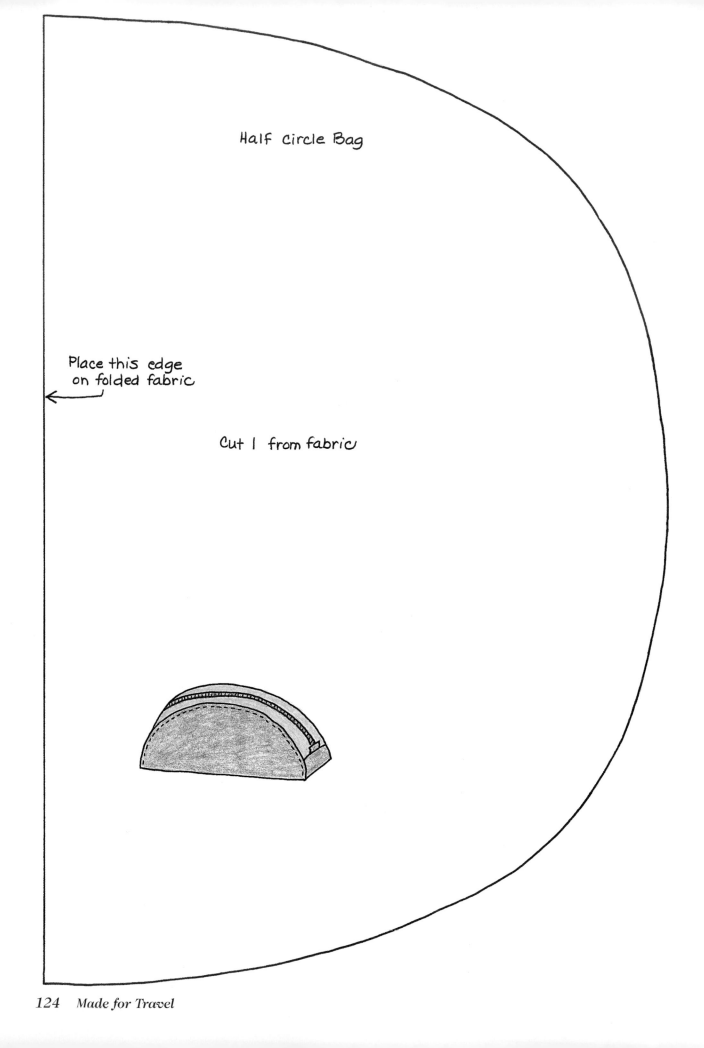

Half circle Bag

Place this edge
on folded fabric

Cut 1 from fabric

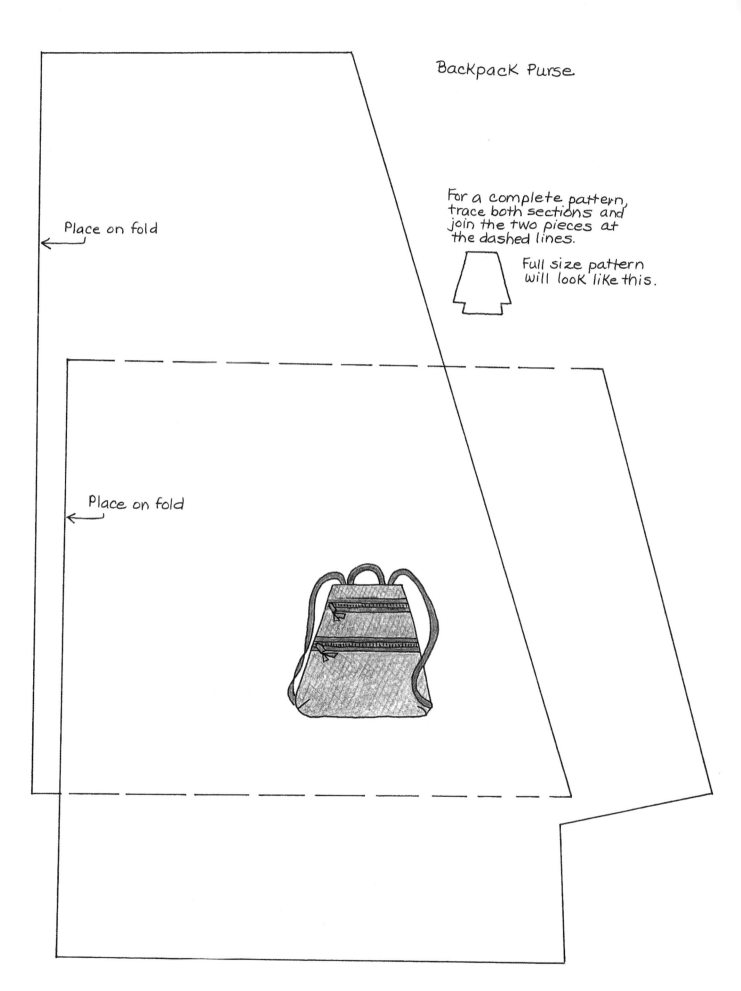

Backpack Purse

Place on fold

For a complete pattern, trace both sections and join the two pieces at the dashed lines.

Full size pattern will look like this.

Place on fold

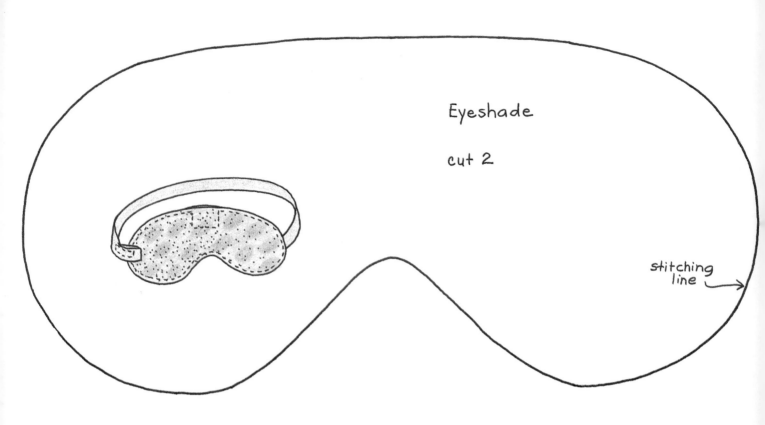

Eyeshade

cut 2

stitching
line

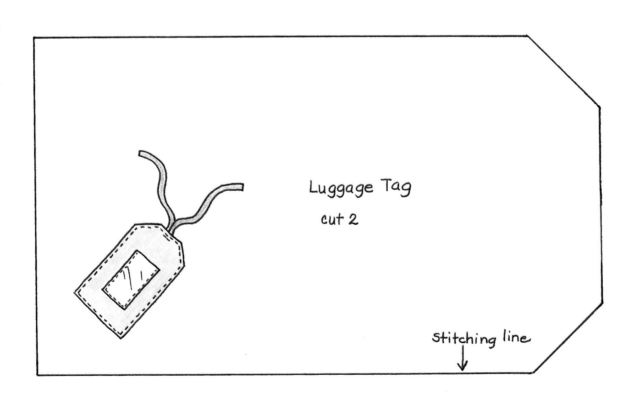

Luggage Tag

cut 2

stitching line

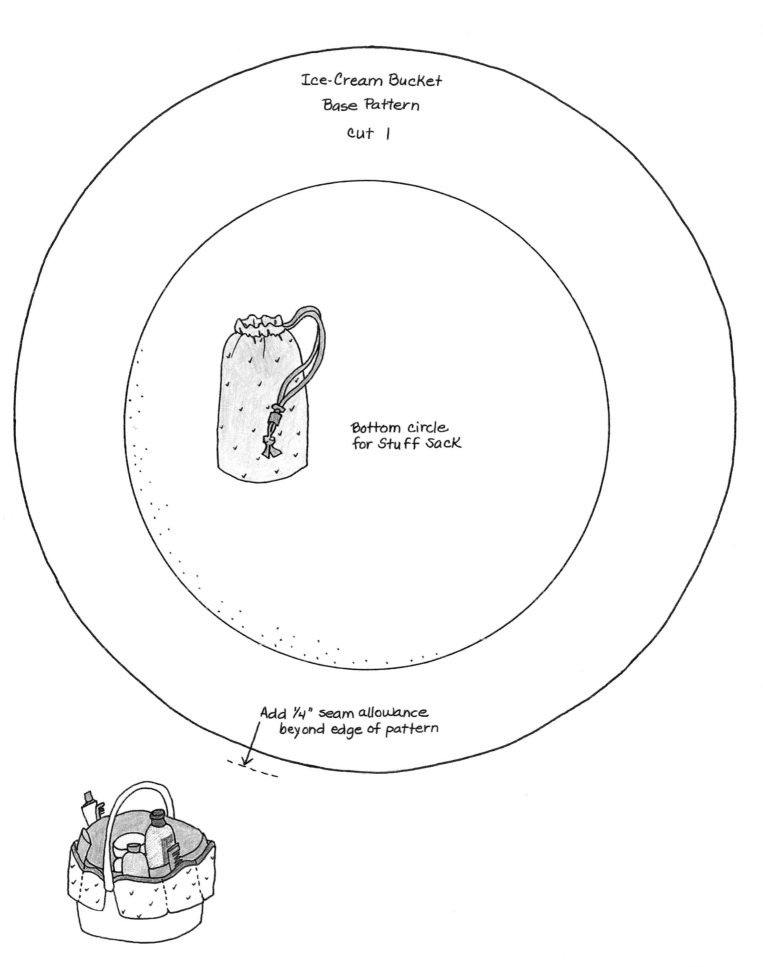

Ice-Cream Bucket
Base Pattern

Cut 1

Bottom circle
for Stuff Sack

Add 1/4" seam allowance
beyond edge of pattern

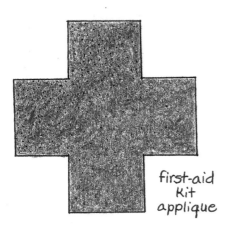

first-aid
Kit
applique

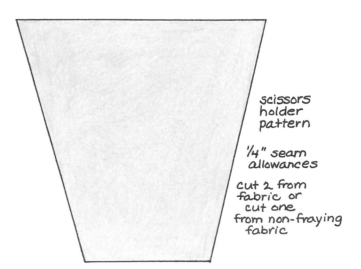

scissors
holder
pattern

1/4" seam
allowances

cut 2 from
fabric or
cut one
from non-fraying
fabric

Travelers' Resources and Websites

Catalog of Sewing Supplies
Clotilde, Inc.
1.800.545.4002
www.clotilde.com

Catalog of Sewing Supplies, including Sensuede
Nancy's Notions
P.O. Box 683
Beaver Dam, WI 53916
1.800.833.0690
www.nancysnotions.com

Ultrasuede and Sensuede
Michiko's Creations
P.O. Box 4313
Napa, CA 94558
www.suedeshop.com

Books, Patterns, Embroidery Cards, and Seminars
Mary Mulari
Mary's Productions
P.O. Box 87-K-4
Aurora, MN 55705
www.marymulari.com
email: mary@marymulari.com

Polarfleece by Malden Mills
mail order source
1.877.289.7652
www.maldenmillsstore.com

Outdoor Fabrics and Supplies
The RainShed, Inc.
707 N. W. 11th
Corvallis, OR 97330
541.753.8900
fax 541.757.1887

Sewing Patterns for Travelers' Vest, Jackets, and More
Saf-T-Pockets
1385 N. W. 49th St.
Portland, OR 97213
www.saf-t-pockets.com

Information About Packing
Smart Packing for Today's Traveler, by Susan Foster
Smart Travel Press
P.O. Box 25514
Portland, OR 97298
www.smartpacking.com

Catalog
America's Leading Source of Travel Supplies
Magellan's
1.800.962.4943
www.magellans.com

Website
Products uniquely well-suited for Travelers
Christine Columbus
1.600.280.4775
www.christinecolumbus.com

Catalog of Clothing and Accessories for Travelers
Norm Thompson
1.800.547.1160
www.normthompson.com